Poetry of Relevance 1

All, all of a piece throughout:
Thy chase had a beast in view;
Thy wars brought nothing about;
Thy lovers were all untrue.
'Tis well an old age is out,
And time to begin a new.
John Dryden
(from *The Secular Masque*)

Poetry of Relevance 1

Homer Hogan

Associate Professor of English
University of Guelph

Special consultant
Kenneth J. Weber
Assistant Professor of English
Ontario College of Education

Methuen

Toronto London
Sydney Wellington

Frontispiece: Bukka White

Library of Congress Catalog Card Number 77-113485

SBN 458 90400 7

Designed by Carl Brett
Printed and bound in Canada
74   73   72   71   70   2   3   4   5

To the Instructor

Poetry of Relevance invites students to find significant connections between poems of our literary heritage and songs that express contemporary interests and concerns. The table of contents makes clear the general strategy: each song lyric is followed by one or more poems that develop the theme or poetic technique found in the lyric.

To take full advantage of this text, the instructor should be sure to play the recommended recording of the song preceding the poems he wishes to discuss. Once a mood is established by the recording, the ways of working from song to poem are limited only by the instructor's ingenuity. The special interest sparked by hearing the songs of such artists as John Lennon, Leonard Cohen, Paul Simon, and Joni Mitchell extends to the poetry itself.

However he proceeds, the instructor should be able to use one or more of the following features of this book: (1) the index of themes, (2) the critical approach developed in the introductions and transitional material, (3) the indexes of poets and song-writers in each volume, and (4) the *Suggestions for Study* prepared for high school students by Kenneth Weber, Assistant Professor of English at the Ontario College of Education. (The *About the Poets* section was also contributed by Professor Weber.)

Complete record information is given with each song and in the discographies at the end of books 1 and 2. Most likely, the instructor will find that about six albums will be all he needs for the semester's work in poetry. Students might be asked to buy or borrow some records of songs not used in class so that they can do independent study.

In comparing books 1 and 2, it will be noticed that although they may be used independently of one another, there are certain advantages in using both. Together they offer a much wider range of songs and poetry. Furthermore, the first volume offers a substantial amount of commentary in the introduction and transitions between sections, whereas the second keeps commentary to a minimum in order to provide a greater number of songs and poems to which the student can apply his own thinking. The introductions to the two books also complement each other. In the first book the introduction is an essay on wonder addressed mainly to the student's affective experience of literature. In the second, the introduction is more intellectually oriented, sketching out certain logical principles that students might use to help settle arguments about literary interpretations. Special topics considered in the first book include the forms of poetic development (1 *Folk Songs and Blues);* the perspectives and philosophy of New Generation songwriters (3 *Tim Buckley);* contexts of imagery (4 *Joni Mitchell);* uses of ambiguity (5 *John Lennon and the Beatles);* surrealism (11 *Robin Williamson);* and the function of myth (12 *Myth and The Ballad of Frankie Lee and Judas Priest).* A model of detailed poetic analysis is offered in the discussion of Joni Mitchell's song-poems. The relation of truth to art is touched upon in connection with an analysis of the blues in the second book (2 *John KaSandra).*

In order to make *Poetry of Relevance* useful to young people who wish to write their own songs and poems, I place particular emphasis on the ways that poetry and song *move* an audience and keep technical terminology at an absolute minimum. I also include song lyrics and poems that vary considerably in quality and effectiveness so that instructors can challenge students to discover why one song or poem works better than another.

Contemporary Canadian, British, and American poetry accounts for about half of the poems in the books; the remainder represent the major periods of British and North American poetic literature. Some of the contemporary poems are by high school and college students. Of special importance is the attention paid to the poetry of the black people of North America. The books include not only some powerful examples of traditional blues lyrics and songs by Jerry Moore, Bukka White, John KaSandra, and the Rev. F. D. Kirkpatrick, but also poems by Langston Hughes, Gwendolyn Brooks, Bob Kaufman, Margaret Walker, Dudley Randall, Robert J. Abrams, Donald Jeffrey Hayes, Calvin C. Hernton, M. Carl Holman, Lucy Smith, Paul Vesey, and Dr. Martin Luther King, whose oratory, as I hope to show, often rises to the level of poetry.

Acknowledgements

With great pleasure, I offer my profound thanks to Joni Mitchell, who first encouraged me to begin this project; my wife, Dorothy, whose musical knowledge was an invaluable resource; Mr. Jay Mark, of TRO; and most of all, my friend and colleague, Dr. Eugene Benson, whose imagination and erudition are responsible for some of the happiest combinations of songs and poems in these books, especially in the sections on John Lennon and Leonard Cohen.

H.H.
University of Guelph
March, 1970

Contents

The Sense of Wonder

"But if I *study* poetry, I won't *enjoy* it!"

There's truth in that objection. Who can thrill to a love affair while he examines it? How can a magician astound us if he tells us his secrets before he does his tricks? Like love affairs and magic shows, poems should be allowed simply to happen to us if we are to experience the first flavors of their delight. But suppose one wants to know how to win a girl's heart, amaze an audience with legerdemain, or— and there's not much difference—write poems and songs? Obviously he will have to do some thinking about how love, magic, or poetry *works*.

The present book is written primarily for this second kind of individual—specifically, the person who wants not merely to consume poetry, as if it were breakfast cereal or cigarettes or some other commodity that people foist on him, but rather to find ways of expressing what *he* is, and what *he* thinks and feels. This reader knows instinctively that writing songs and poems would be one of the best means available for opening a way out for his mind and emotions. He will also understand that mastering the liberating arts of song and poetry is not easy (if it were, they would not be so dearly prized). He will accept the fact that these arts must not only be studied, but also deeply, even at times painfully thought about.

It does not follow,however, that poets and artists, who struggle for mastery of their craft, thereby destroy their ability to enjoy it. The fact is that understanding the marvellous working of their art gives artists a deeply aware enjoyment that makes their work the center of their lives.

By also making it possible for consumers of poems and songs to imagine what goes into "growing" them, *Poetry of Relevance* should enable casual readers and listeners to heighten their experience and to approach, at least indirectly, the love of the artist for his craft. Yet, there will remain the problem created by the fact that enjoying poems and songs cannot take place at the same time they are being studied. The answer is that the listener and reader must learn, like the artist, to shift roles: to be, at one time, the audience that surrenders to the work, then next, the creator who releases it. If he does this, each change of role will be accompanied by an awareness, in the background, of what was previously learned so that in the process of alternating between audience and creator, he will become increasingly sensitive in both capacities.

But how shall we begin our study? We might have introduced students to the workings of poetry by fixing a "definition" for poetry—a dangerous business—and then dissected the elements of poems, mainly plot, character-ization, thought, imagery, diction, tone, style, rhythm, sound, and so on. Such information is valuable; but since it is so widely available, we will concentrate here and in the body of the text on something that is not so fully discussed, namely, the question of contexts. The most important of these is the *context of wonder.*

To cast people into a state of wonder—that is, to astound, amaze, enchant or just quietly charm them—is the basic challenge for the poet, as well as for the composer, juggler, showman, or in fact anyone whose work is tempting others to play. People do not let the poet meet this challenge easily. They insist that he entice their imaginations before they surrender to him. Of course, a writer may say he's not interested in amazing or charming others, that he wants only to express himself. But in this case he becomes his own audience and is doomed to work for a taskmaster who can be far more severe than those "outside," as external judges can never make their needs and demands so intimately known. In fact, it is so much more difficult to please one's self deeply and permanently that the best poetry is usually that which comes out of this attempt. We can thus formulate this rule: to move others, aim primarily to move yourself. The poet can find humanity within himself far more effectively than he can by trying to calculate objectively how strangers will react to what he does—and the strangers will confirm this by their actual responses. Whether, then, the poet writes immediately for others, or better, indirectly by being their representative, he needs to know above all the dynamics of wonder, the *raison d'être* of his craft. Instinctively, of course, the accomplished artist knows them very well, but for those who are just starting to create, it is well to state them explicitly.

There are five aspects of wonder: perceiving, apprehending unity, surprise, engagement, and discovery. They operate in reality as a totally fused, self-developing process. They all make one another possible and can be separated only artifically for purposes of study.

Perceiving
Wonder is most intense when we are most engrossed in the object of wonder and least aware of our subjective reactions. A poet will spoil his poem if he allows his feeling to get in the way of what evokes feelings in his reader, namely, clearly illuminated objects and striking situations. In brief, the poet can destroy feelings by letting them dominate and cloud over their sources.

Uncontrolled emotion in the poet leads him to neglect the emotional requirements of his audience when it stampedes him into mentioning feelings instead of creating them, or when the urgency of giving it release tempts him to wrap feelings hurriedly in vagueness, generality, dull, first-come ideas, or old brown-paper clichés. He might, for example, try to make us wonder at the variety of beauty in nature by exclaiming, in his passion: "Oh, how my heart throbs when I behold the glory of all the different colors under God's heaven!"—a line which employs all the feeling-killers just mentioned plus the deadly device of wordiness, the engulfing of significance in an excess of sound. Consider, by way of contrast, the opening lines of Gerard Manley Hopkins' poem *Pied Beauty:*

Glory be to God for dappled things—
   For skies of couple-colour as a brinded cow;
     For rose-moles all in stipple upon trout that swim

Hopkins *shows* us the variety of colors instead of just referring to it, and he makes it interesting by focusing on a special, seldom used term for color variety—dappledness —which in turn is linked to an unlikely combination of God, skies, cow, "rose-moles," and trout. Who would normally associate roses with moles, or think of fusing them together as a way of identifying the red spots on brook trout? Hopkins also lifts his material out of usualness in these lines by means of exploding phrases, syncopated rhythm, compressed diction, and exciting sound —all manifesting, rather than being overcome by the intensity of faith and insight which, of course, is the ultimate source of his poem's power.

Although the ordinary is the poet's natural enemy, we should not conclude that it must therefore never appear in poetry. On the contrary, it is essential for the ordinary to be there when the poet needs to begin where his listeners are, or to bring them back where they can rest before making another climb with him, to let them feel the relevance of his magic for their daily existence. In fact, the art of popular song consists, at its best, in paying ordinary life the closest sort of attention. In doing so, the songwriter treats the language of everyday-ness, including clichés, slang, and the easy idioms of conversation, as something not to escape, but rather to exploit in order that he may carry out the special assignment that makes him a songwriter, the task of rescuing the ordinary from itself. Here is a brief characterization of this rescue work: normally, the daydreams and experiences of routine living, working, and loving simply come and go; the songwriter arrests the flow and isolates some of the dreams and experiences in forms that suddenly give them a special and enduring significance.

During the course of this book, we will have more to say about how (and in what sense) this transformation takes place in contemporary song. To prevent misunderstanding, however, it is wise to note at once that the significance of ordinary life which a songwriter uncovers may be on one level the very insignificance of that life. Telling the story of the deserted Marcie, Joni Mitchell writes: "Marcie's faucet needs a plumber/Marcie's sorrow needs a man"—a gentle ironic stroke that brings out sharply a special kind of bleakness possible in common life that common life blurs. John Lennon goes much further in *A Day in the Life,* a song which concerns the emptiness, not just in one person's life, but in that of a contemporary Everyman; an emptiness, furthermore, that is found on every side of daily existence. What makes this hollowness ring for us is the way Lennon manages vaguely articulate, cliché-ridden, colloquial language. The opening line—"I read the news today oh boy"—is an example of one of Lennon's favorite devices for making this language and the dullness it expresses an object of wonder for us. The technique consists of making unusual combinations of usual phrases. Linking "I read the news today" with "oh boy," Lennon levels out the enthusiasm of "oh boy" and makes us wonder about the quality of the speaker's peculiar, flat thrills. Equally odd juxtapositions of routine phrases in the following lines both increase our curiosity and feed it with disturbing bits of revelation, until finally we are made ready for the weirdest combination of all—the fusion of life-affirmation and life-negation in the interminable tonic chord upon which the song finally dissolves.

Apprehending Unity

We now come to the second aspect of wonder—apprehending unity. It grows in the form of an ever-widening system of expectations, which in turn sets up a unified world in which events gain significance. How can the poet stimulate this growth? One simple way is to focus on the movement of a single image, the course of which sucks in, as it were, as much as the moving image can carry without dragging.

In Robert Graves' poem, *The Legs,* the poet stands in the rain watching the legs of human traffic going up and down

a road "resolutely nowhere/in both directions." He laughs
at the "senseless, frightening/fate of being legs" until he
suddenly wonders whether he too might be "a walker/
from the knees down," at which point his legs run away
with him and carry him through "twenty puddles" before
he regains control over them. As can be seen even from
this brief summary, the central image in Graves' poem is
not only about movement, but also in movement. Watching
the legs of the crowd hurrying in meaningless patterns, we
understand the poet's amusement at the loss of purpose
and individuality in modern society; but understanding
this, we then also perceive how right the poet is in includ-
ing himself in the picture he sees, and, indirectly, his
readers as well. The image of the moving legs leads
inexorably, then, to what is literally a kinesthetic revelation
of the way society destroys our identity.

Amy Lowell's poem, *Patterns,* provides growing unity by
means of a more complex device—the use of an expand-
ing concept. Beginning with the pattern of "garden paths,"
the poem adds the patterns of fashionable dress, upper-
class decorum, military procedure, and war, climaxing in
the cry, "Christ! What are patterns for?" And unifying all
these surface patterns is the hidden one made by a woman
struggling to keep her balance in the face of news about
her fiancé's death.

Returning to John Lennon's *A Day in the Life,* we can see
that this song reveals a principle of unity in its very title,
but for a sharper idea of what is going on, we should
consider the similarity of action represented in each verse.
Then we will see a strange thing about the "life" being led
by the speaker and the crowds he talks about: the life
consists of images of life refracted through newspapers,
films, books, and show business; that is, the life is totally
inauthentic. More subtly than either Graves or Lowell,
Lennon leads us to look for unity on many different levels
of his song through the cross relations of characters,
actions, thoughts, phrases, music, and attitudes.

Surprise

Surprise, the third aspect of wonder, belongs to the emotional side of it, whereas the apprehension of unity is a function of wonder as an intellectual activity. As we noted earlier, our natural craving for the unexpected both contradicts and requires the maintenance of the unexpected; without the unity that comes from satisfying a system of expectations, a poem or song may shock or irritate, but not, in an aesthetic sense, really surprise.

Wilfred Owen's anti-war poem, *Dulce et Decorum Est,* illustrates well the balance required. Beginning by comparing his fellow soldiers to "old beggars under sacks," Owen gradually increases the repulsiveness of his imagery, finally asking us to hear, after a gas attack,

... at every jolt, the blood
Come gargling from the froth-corrupted lungs,
Bitter as the cud
Of vile, incurable sores on innocent tongues.

These gory details shake us; but we want to be shaken because Owen has shown us that he is "telling it like it is." Our natural love of truth has been aroused, and it demands that the facts be seen, no matter how they hurt.

At another extreme, Robin Williamson offers almost no preparation for this couplet occurring mid-way through *The Mad Hatter's Song:*

Prometheus the problem child still juggling with his
brains
Gives his limping leopard's visions to the miser in his
veins

But still these wild phrases surprise rather than shock because we've come to expect that in this song, lines will not follow one another clearly. In other words, the illogic of madness in this lyric becomes itself a kind of logic guiding our expectations.

Seeking both the expected, for the sake of the intellect, and the unexpected, for the sake of emotion, wonder thus seems to be self-contradictory. The conflict between these

opposing tendencies is that which impels wonder, just as
the tension between negative and positive charges is that
which makes electrical current possible. Also like elec-
tricity, wonder requires that its inner opposing tendencies
be brought close enough to each other so that they
produce a conflict, and yet not so close that one side can
ever win. In poetry the best example of this positioning of
opposites is the paradox, a statement that at first seems
self-contradictory and then on further inspection seems
to state a truth. Consider the sentence: "Man is the most
intelligent and the most brutal of animals." "Intelligent"
and "brutal" almost contradict each other but not com-
pletely, for "brutal" may denote cruelty and ferocity as
well as stupidity. Thinking about this distinction, we then
see that these terms do not merely co-exist with each
other—they are, in fact, intimately linked, for it is precisely
man's superior intelligence that enables him to be more
viciously destructive than any other animal.

More generally conceived, paradoxes are not limited to
particular statements. Paradoxical effects can be created
also by means of plot construction, characterization,
argument, and, as in many of the Beatles' songs, the
contrasting of music and words. The first line and title of
E. E. Cummings' poem, *pity this busy monster, manunkind,*
is a good example of indirect but complex paradox. Using
the coined word, "manunkind," instead of "mankind,"
Cummings forces us to ask in what way man is *un*-kind.
Our answer must be not simply that man lacks generosity;
Cummings has spoken of man as a "monster," which
leads us to infer that "unkind" means "unnatural," that is,
not true to kind or species. But how is it possible for an
animal to be untrue to its own nature? The question does
not make sense—and yet there is one animal that might
very well be said to live in this condition: man, the animal
whose business is to turn everything into machinery,
including himself. We leave it to the reader to see how the
poem unfolds this paradox without ever violating the basic
rule that surprise and rightness be fused.

Tim Buckley's *No Man Can Find the War* is an example of a whole song built on one paradox. In this case, the paradox is the final line of each verse. It surprises because it apparently contradicts the lines leading up to it, that describe all the places where men seem to have no trouble at all finding war. The line is convincing, however, because it makes us realize that if men had really *found* war, they would have destroyed it just as they would a mad dog. When we see the hidden truth in the statement, we do not therefore stop our wondering, for that truth prompts us to keep looking for the real sources of our affliction. Thus the tension between disturbance and understanding is preserved.

The model of the paradox can be applied to the development of poems and songs as well as to the impact of important moments in them. From what has been said, it is probably already evident that the best, that is, the most wonder-provoking ending is that which is both most startling, and yet, on further thought, most likely, given what has preceded it—a point made by Aristotle long ago. For such an ending to take place, the development must have a certain character. In the first place, tension between the expected and unexpected should mount gradually toward successive peaks, each higher than its predecessor —"higher" because more surprising and portentous— and, of course, there must be valleys of rest between the peaks. The reason for this pattern is simply the demands of the human nervous system, which must be met before feeling can be increased by means of art. In brief, the principle behind the pattern is that in art, emotion must be built up *incrementally*. Secondly, the development should be such that the ending is felt to grow out of the beginning, not only naturally, but also in a way that exhausts all significant potentialities of surprise and unity found there. In a good ball game, all the conflicts that develop are potential in the very beginning, and by the end of the game, these have all been worked through; that is, every player has done his best. An analogous situation is found

in poems and lyrics. In brief, then, if poetry is to develop in
wonder, it must do so *logically, surprisingly, fully,* and
incrementally.

A simple but powerful example of full development can
be found in the gospel song beginning, "Death don't have
no mercy in this land." The last line is the same as the first,
but by the time we reach it, its impact has been greatly
increased, for each verse gives another instance of how
the truth of this statement will affect us personally; Death
taking away our mother, then our father, then our sister,
then our brother, then everybody. Although we protest
against the prophecy of each verse, our protests only
heighten our sense of the inescapable tyranny of death.

The old English *Cherry Tree Carol* is a complex case of
development that is logical and surprising as well as full.
The problem in the carol is to make a miraculous ending
seem both astonishing and credible. To establish credi-
bility—which is a kind of conformity with expectations—
the carol realistically portrays a reaction of the man
Joseph, who knows he could not be the father of the child
his wife Mary is carrying. She asks him for cherries—a
realistic detail of pregnancy—and he replies, "Let the
father of the baby gather cherries for thee!" Knowing that
God would take some means to overcome Joseph's natural
suspicions, we understand when Christ speaks from
within Mary's womb: "Bend down the tallest tree that my
mother might have some." Although understandable,
God's act is still a miracle, a violation of natural order by
divine intervention. Furthermore, the great import of the
truth it declares sharply contrasts with the simple, homely
circumstances surrounding it. Thus, though the ending
seems an inevitable and complete resolution of what is
given in Joseph's natural suspicions and God's goodness
and power, it is also a complex surprise, suspending us
between charm and awe.

Tim Buckley's song, *Morning-Glory,* illustrates both the
principles of logical, full, and surprising development, and

that of incremental tension. The speaker in the song tells of his encounter with a "Hobo" whom he wished desperately to hear old "Stories" from, but whom he was too afraid to trust. The Hobo, seeing that the speaker has a closed heart, walks away, refusing to give the words the speaker seeks. The last verse to this suggestive allegory is as follows:

> "Then you be damned!" I screamed to the Hobo,
> "Leave me alone," I wept to the Hobo;
> "Turn into stone," I knelt to the Hobo;
> And he walked away from my fleeting house.

Consider the sequence of emotional peaks here: anger, grief, adoration, each one more surprising than its predecessor. The rapid alternation between these extremes is also surprising, both in itself and because of the abrupt increase in pacing it brings. The result is like three skyrockets ending a fireworks display: the first shoots far higher than anything else in the show, the second even higher, and the third, highest of all. Good poetry and good showmanship are closely allied. In both, the problem is to raise wonder bit by bit until one has generated enough tension to make it explode.

Engagement

We turn now to the fourth aspect of wonder—engagement. Though difficult to explain, the process is simple enough. In the case of poetry, if there is nothing suggestive in the poem, nothing to make us bring to it our emotional and intellectual experiences, no wonder will be evoked by the poem either. On the other hand, if it is so vague that we can use it to express whatever we wish, the poem will have no challenge and hence will also lack wonder—or at least will eventually lose it. A good poem, in other words, should let us in, but not to take it over.

But what happens to us when we are inside an effective poem? In *Dover Beach,* Matthew Arnold writes that the "Sea of Faith" is now

Retreating to the breath
Of the night-wind down the vast edges drear
And naked shingles of the world.

By means of this metaphor, he engages our senses and imagination to such an extent that we can feel the chilling significance of man's growing loss of faith in God. He also indirectly invites our intellect to check out what he is saying, to find examples of disillusionment with religion in those around us and in ourselves. Through suggestion, made emphatic by compression of detail, Arnold makes it possible for us to become partners with him, as it were, in the creation of his poem. A poet who merely lectures us prevents this engagement and so restricts the possibilities for wonder.

On the other hand, if we are truly inside a poem, whatever we bring, we bring *to* and *for* it so that the poem can be fully realized for what it is. The bitterly anti-war song, *Johnny, I Hardly Knew Yeh,* is rich with humour, but if we don't understand that this is Irish black humor, we will laugh where there should be tears of indignation and thereby destroy the work. Our task is to re-create in our minds the feeling and vision of the woman in the song who sees her broken husband returning home from a war. We must share with her the peculiar fusion of anger, horror, and the struggle for self-control that sustains her terrible irony. This work of re-creation and active sharing is still *our* activity, of course, and though it is undertaken for something outside of ourselves, we find, if the poem or song is a good one, that in doing this work we uncover depths of feeling and understanding within us that we never knew existed.

In the preceding remarks we stressed the obligations of the reader. The implication for the writer is that his work must be such as to compel this attention. Perhaps the greatest artistic merit of *Johnny, I Hardly Knew Yeh* is just its capacity to do this by activating our deepest feelings. At the same time, however, the writer must be able to limit his appeal in a very important way: he must not let us become so involved with what he is representing that we look upon it exactly as we do real life. In the present case, for example, the horror of Johnny's condition must not seem so vivid that our outrage overcomes our wonder. If that happens we are thrown back into the attitudes we take in real life, attitudes that make us directly relate objects and people to our own personal needs and passions, thereby distorting them and making it difficult to see them as they are apart from our demands. A logician may object that what we are saying here is self-contradictory, for we imply that reality is made unreal by reality and real by unreality (art). We admit the implication, but we would claim it to be one of the many paradoxes of aesthetics rather than a total self-contradiction. For an example of its cogency, we would point once again to Lennon's *A Day in the Life,* in which the reality of everyday life becomes clear precisely because of the ingenious ways by which Lennon keeps his listeners at a distance from it.

Discovery

The fifth dimension of wonder to be considered is wonder as discovery. In reading poems, we find our interest increasing as we see the possibilities of the opening lines develop from verse to verse. The good poet plants the seeds of possibilities in the very beginning of his work and then lets them grow enticingly until, at the end of the work, the reader suddenly sees the mature flower. But he makes sure that these possibilities are intrinsically interesting and that the work grows naturally out of them, and not merely out of obedience to his will. No formula can be given for locating ideas with intrinsic interest or for characterizing exactly the way a given idea can most effectively and naturally grow. Here the poet can rely only on his intuition. We notice one thing about how this intuition operates, however, when it is most effective. Like the composer who writes a good melody, the poet proceeds best when he *listens* for what must come next. He should become, in other words, an instrument of his vision. What he tries to tune into are the unseen, unheard, unthought potentials of beauty in the germ of an idea. Though these potentials are in a kind of limbo, they are nevertheless extremely exacting. A composer can go wrong—and hear himself go wrong—by giving a note one beat instead of two; a poet can spend a sleepless night looking for just the right word demanded by the specific pattern of beauty to which he is committed. When, however, he finds a good idea and is able to surrender to it, to sense everything going right, then, as the ancients put it, he may know the ecstasy of being possessed by the gods. More important, from our point of view, is the fact that his listeners too can share in that ecstasy as the unfolding idea takes them over, revealing its beautiful possibilities according to the laws of its own distinctive nature.

We speak of a mysterious business here that is the very center of poetic creation, and our abstract terms may seem applicable only to "great" literature. But wonder as the discovery of possibilities can take place in experiencing even a simple song. Listening to Tim Buckley's *Once I Was* is immediately gratifying because we sense the simple beauty of its idea and the perfect way each line follows the other in the development of the song. The idea or germ of the song is basically this: a boy laments his rejection by the girl he loves by expressing himself with utter simplicity, dignity, and gentle poignancy. Why this idea is potentially beautiful cannot be fully explained: all we can do is to point perhaps to the intrinsic loveliness of the unique combination of qualities characterizing the boy's lament. Nor can the rightness of each succeeding line be proven or totally accounted for. Consider, for example, the chorus:

> And sometimes I wonder
> Just for awhile
> Will you ever remember me

If someone were to say that this is dull or maudlin, all we could do is ask him to listen to Buckley sing these lines (they must, of course, be sung in order to work). If he still failed to perceive their tender beauty after hearing Buckley, our only recourse would be to persuade him to have his nervous system checked.

Of course, some beautiful poems are more logically defensible than others. Robert Frost's *Acquainted with the Night* can easily be defended as a natural and complete elaboration of the connotations in the first line or opening idea: "I have been one acquainted with the night." Yet, how far can we explain the working power of the famous moon-image, for example, the "one luminary clock against the sky"? Admittedly, a great deal can be said about its appropriateness, but its real power could obviously not be communicated to one whom the moon never frightened.

Self-developing process

We come at last to the final observation we made about wonder. We pointed out that the aspects we have discussed are not in fact distinguished during the course of experiencing wonder; rather, they are all elements in what is felt to be a homogenous, self-developing process. In the various cases we have cited to illustrate our remarks, we could often have demonstrated the effect of any aspect of wonder by means of the same example. Hopkins' lines make us perceive "dappled things" because they relate them to a unified world-picture, surprise us by paradoxical juxtapositions, engage our senses and imagination, and uncover unique possibilities of beauty. On the other hand, these causes of heightened perception would be inoperative if "dappled things" were not in themselves worth seeing.

The intimate connections among all these aspects of wonder suggest one way of offering "explanations" of songs and poems. Realizing that a work of art is a self-developing process in which an artist tries to bring certain materials into the full light of wonder, we can simply ask, in any particular case, (1) What are we supposed to wonder *about?* and (2) How are we tempted to wonder about it? The object of wonder will include, of course, not merely what is imitated—a situation, action, character, philosophical or ethical truth, natural or social scenery— but also the cluster of feelings associated with these materials—pity, sadness, fear, anger, indignation, disgust, joy and so on. Nor is there any clear limit to the range of feelings that can be in an object of wonder. In principle, the adverb "wonderfully" can be attached to practically any feeling. To cite a highly debatable case, Andy Worhol has produced a movie of a skyscraper in which there is nothing but a continual changeless picture of the building against the sky, the result of which is supposed to be not just boring, but wonderfully boring. The one aesthetic necessity is that whatever the feelings expressed or evoked in a work of art, they must be presented in such a way that it is in wonder they are ultimately received. If a work of imagination leaves us merely angry, or otherwise unhappy with its material, we obviously will not return to it; and if it leaves us merely attracted to the material, as in the case of successful pornography and TV commercials, then we will want the "real thing" and be discontent with its imitation.

How we are tempted to wonder about the objects presented by works of art can be reduced, perhaps, to two considerations: (1) inclusion of materials and feelings that are in themselves interesting to us as human beings (rather than, say, as accountants, engineers, taxpayers, and so forth); and (2) the presentation of these elements according to the techniques discussed in the course of this essay.

We consider now the contents of this book, popular songs and poems. Popular song has always come in many varieties, though today it takes more shapes than ever before—folk, blues, rock, calypso, western, raga, jazz, straight pop, and all combinations thereof, bearing labels like "urban," "rural," "cool," "heavy," "African," "acid," "funky," "put-down," "protest," and so on ad infinitum. For our purposes, however, one basic division is crucial; namely, that between what we shall call "authentic" and "inauthentic" popular song. The first kind attempts to do justice to the rhythms, joys, sorrows, and dreams of ordinary life. When it fails in this attempt, people call it "sincere" but bad. The second kind tries to dull us to ordinary life as it is by soothing us into accepting a glossy, synthetic substitute. It is merely commercial, escapist, and "phony". When it succeeds, those whom it does not fool may admit that it is good, but will insist that it is still just "slick merchandise".

Poetry of Relevance includes only what we believe to be "authentic" popular song—that which tries, more or less successfully, to be *relevant* to everyday existence. It also invites students to find connections between these songs and formal poems. One reason for the invitation is that we think students may discover many ways in which poems can be as relevant as popular songs to their present interests and in some cases, at least, even more so, since included in the interests of young people particularly is a desire for experience that is thoroughly extraordinary, a desire more likely to be satisfied by pure poetry than by songs. Another reason is that students who are poets or songwriters themselves can learn a great deal about the two arts by carefully comparing them. The lyricist can find, for example, the limits and possibilities of lyric-writing as he sees what words can do when they are freed from music; and the poet can gain an insight into what is really essential in poetry when he hears what words can do within the severe limits set by melody.

In the course of these comparisons, a fundamental dispute may arise between the lyric writer and the poet. The question is who has chosen the better art? At first glance, it would seem that the poet could easily win the argument. Doubtlessly, popular lyrics must be considerably simpler than poems, confined as they are to expressing ordinary life within the discipline of music. Furthermore, lyrics in themselves are normally weaker than poems, their rhythms, sound effects, and arrangements of lines—their *prosody*—being less daring and frequently even boring.

Lyrical diction and sentence structure are also relatively weaker. In songs, words, phrases, and sentences tend to be sparse and light, whereas in poems they can be made to thunder with significance.

There are some good points, however, that a songwriter may make in his defense. In the first place, he can cite the obvious fact that a song or poem can be experienced fully only if we hear the song well-*sung* and the poem well-*spoken*. Only after that condition is met, he will say, can we make a judgment, and then the fair question to ask is whether it is songs or poems that produce the greater *verbal impact* on our sense of wonder. Put that way, the question immediately exposes the groundlessness of some of the objections to lyrics as poetry. For when we hear lyrics sung, as they are intended to be, they can produce effects of rhythm, sound, and structure which can be at least as complex and interesting as those found in formal poems. Furthermore, when the words and phrases that look so frail on paper are carried by melody, they hover and undulate in the mind, forcing us to attend to all their connotations. The lyricist, in fact, can quite justly challenge the poet to get such attention for his objects of wonder. To make us think about a line in a poem as we do a line in a good song, the poet needs to reach deep into his bag of devices for linguistic emphasis—for highly condensed phrases, twists of syntax, and complex concepts that seize our intellectual curiosity.

A second argument the lyricist could use relates to the most important common task that he shares with the poet. As we pointed out earlier, successful art is that which brings objects of human concern into the light of wonder. Now the lyricist can argue that words alone admit this light only indirectly, as they are in themselves only counters or symbols for things and experiences. Fused with music, however, words are linked to an immediate physical equivalent for sorrow, joy, tenderness, or any other basic emotion they may be expressing, and consequently the songwriter can do a swifter, cleaner, and more accurate job of representing experience. In fairness, we would have to concede that here the lyricist is right, at least in so far as elemental, intensely emotional experience is concerned. Finally, he could with justice also insist that some feelings belong uniquely to music and can only be expressed in song, notably, the blues.

On the other hand, the poet might turn the thrust of these arguments back upon the songwriter. Admitting the greater difficulty he has in relying solely on words for rhythm, sound, attention-holding devices, and the revelation of sensuous or passionate experience, he could say in reply that his listeners only applaud him the more when he meets this challenge, that he is more of a wonder-worker. He could also claim to be more of a magician since he must draw music out of the words themselves. Finally, he might add that there are feelings over which he too can assert sole stewardship, namely, those belonging to the activity of complex imagining which only speech can express.

But we will not take sides. We will only say that neither the songwriter nor the poet appears to be totally victorious and that what is most important about the possible dispute we've been describing is the way it brings the work of each into perspective. If the reader will check out the arguments advanced by each side through listening to the songs and speaking the poems in this book, he will discover, for example, not only the power of lyrics as a source for verbal impact, despite their slight appearance, but also much about what a poet must do with rhythm, sound, and words to match what music does for good songs. In addition, he will see how lyrics, by virtue of their greater simplicity, sharply reveal the basic elements of pure poetry, and how poems, because of their greater flexibility, develop the potentialities of these elements.

In concluding, it may be useful to view the relations of poetry and song in an historical context. When man first

created poetry, he did not write it or speak it; he *sang* it.
What prompted him to poetry was the beat of drums, the
wild sound of stringed instruments, and the rhythms and
cries of his people dancing around him. In other words,
poetry was born in what was in all essentials the basic
rock experience. For thousands of years poetry did very
well there. Bards fashioned the great epics of Europe,
Asia, and Africa with the aid of lyres and the other
ancestors of the guitar, and one old string-picker from
Greece managed to compose the greatest poems of all
time, the *Iliad* and the *Odyssey*. Then civilization arrived;
music and poetry split, and in keeping with the laws of
technological growth, became ever more complex
and specialized.

Today, the re-emergence of the old relation of poetry
and music and people may eventually restore something
of this ancient glory of poetry. That is why our new
"age of rock" may be culturally of the highest importance.
But although this can be dismissed as mere speculation,
there is an important technical fact which cannot be
denied: the new rock rhythms have freed lyricists of the
necessity to fit words to rigid melodic patterns and thereby
opened the door to a vast range of lyrical possibilities.
Rock music can carry nearly any poetic material—just as
long as it can be chanted.

One warning: pains have been taken in this book *not*
to include only the very best songs and poems. It is
impossible to understand the grounds for effectiveness in
lyric writing and poetry unless one sees how it varies and
then tries to account for these variations. Consequently the
songs and poems here vary in quality. We think, for
instance, that there might be some question about the
selection from Shakespeare included in the "Folk Songs
and Blues" section when it is compared to the fusion of
lyrics, music, and singing represented by Rev. Gary Davis'
performance of *Death Don't Have No Mercy*. Of course,
to raise such questions, we must be bold enough to
be heretical.

poetry and song in an historical context. When man first created poetry, he did not write it or speak it; he *sang* it. What prompted him to poetry was the beat of drums, the wild sound of stringed instruments, and the rhythms and cries of his people dancing around him. In other words, poetry was born in what was in all essentials the basic rock experience. For thousands of years poetry did very well there. Bards fashioned the great epics of Europe, Asia, and Africa with the aid of lyres and the other ancestors of the guitar, and one old string-picker from Greece managed to compose the greatest poems of all time, the *Iliad* and the *Odyssey*. Then civilization arrived; music and poetry split, and in keeping with the laws of technological growth, became ever more complex and specialized.

Today, the re-emergence of the old relation of poetry and music and people may eventually restore something of this ancient glory of poetry. That is why our new "age of rock" may be culturally of the highest importance. But although this can be dismissed as mere speculation, there is an important technical fact which cannot be denied: the new rock rhythms have freed lyricists of the necessity to fit words to rigid melodic patterns and thereby opened the door to a vast range of lyrical possibilities. Rock music can carry nearly any poetic material—just as long as it can be chanted.

One warning: pains have been taken in this book *not* to include only the very best songs and poems. It is impossible to understand the grounds for effectiveness in lyric writing and poetry unless one sees how it varies and then tries to account for these variations. Consequently the songs and poems here vary in quality. We think, for instance, that there might be some question about the selection from Shakespeare included in the "Folk Songs and Blues" section when it is compared to the fusion of lyrics, music, and singing represented by Rev. Gary Davis' performance of *Death Don't Have No Mercy*. Of course, to raise such questions, we must be bold enough to be heretical.

Overleaf: Rev. Gary Davis

1

Folk Songs and Blues

In contrast to the contemporary song-poem, which is highly personal and individualistic, the folk song distills the experiences of generations of men and women. It is not the particular, but the generic man who sings, and a good folk performer will bear the mark of his whole tribe. His song is his own, but it is also the song of his people. Since the folk tradition is an oral rather than a written one, the folk singer learns his material from people around him. The songs are handed down from generation to generation, and in the course of traveling from one singer to another, through different regions of the country, across oceans and centuries, the folk song becomes altered, regionalized, and personalized. The folk song, living in this way, is reduced to essentials. Only the most fundamental characteristics of poetry and song allow it to survive. Therefore, by taking a good look at folk songs, we should be able to clarify what we should look for when we examine the workings of any song or poem.

Analysis of lyrics and poems begins, of course, with the identification of what they are *about*. What a work is about can be called its "object of wonder," a fusion of subject matter and associated feelings (see General Introduction). The trick is first to spot the object from a view of the work as a whole so that nothing is left out. This means that our initial description should be very simple and general. It also means that we should look most carefully at the title, the opening line, and the very last words, for these are the places where a good poet or lyricist will often give his object its greatest emphasis. Proceeding this way, we might, for example, characterize the object of wonder in *Black Is the Color* as the beauty of a lover, in *Stackerlee* as the attractiveness of a bad man, and in *Death Don't Have No Mercy* as the fearsomeness of death. The next step would be to describe the details of the object, being careful, of course, to preserve their relative emphasis in the poem or song, as it is by means of his system of emphases that an artist hopes to control our system of expectations.

After locating the object of wonder, we look for the ways the poem or song attempts to make us regard it as such. Here we can distinguish four major kinds of techniques: those associated with (1) the object of wonder itself, (2) the work presenting it, (3) the writer, and (4) the audience. In practice, these techniques actually involve all four entities, but one will normally be more prominent than the others.

The first kinds of techniques establish the intrinsic interest of the content. The quality of blackness is, in itself, a major source of the charm in *Black Is the Color;* and *Death Don't Have No Mercy in This Land* derives its fundamental power, of course, from the terrible truth it expresses.

The techniques of the second sort are the most complicated. They concern the management of the central tension between the expected and unexpected that impels the process of wonder. Basically, the writer's means for developing this conflict include *drama, narration, argument,* and *description.* In *drama,* we actually hear or see the conflict taking place between and within characters in a problem situation. The dialogue portions of *The Cherry Tree Carol* both exemplify drama and indicate the limits of its use. As it is the most vivid means of developing conflict, pure drama is normally reserved in poetry for only the most important moments. In *narration,* conflict that could be dramatic is filtered through a third person who tells us about an action. *Stackerlee* and *John Henry,* which are primarily narrations, demonstrate that what narrative form lacks in intensity it gains in range, for by virtue of their narrators, these ballads are free to unify far greater quantities of diverse materials than drama is capable of doing. In *argument*—conceived here broadly as discourse that offers reasons for conclusions—conflict is refracted still further. The opposition in this case is presented as taking place in the realm of ideas. But this does not mean that argument is an aesthetically weak form. On the contrary, the very distance it puts between us and immediate reality enables argument to handle subject matter far too strong for drama and narration; *Death Don't Have No Mercy* would be unbearable if it were dramatized. In *description,* conflict would seem to be operating in its most reflected form. Descriptive discourse simply offers observations, and superficially the only tension present is between what is said and what is not said. That tension, however, can be exquisite when the said and the unsaid together express profound thought or, as in *Black Is the Color,* intense feeling.

The third set of techniques for making us wonder about the object of a poem or song, those which we said related to the writer, concerns the positioning of the writer in relation to his object of wonder, the work itself, and his audience. Even in ballads like *Stackerlee* and *John Henry,* the attitude of the writer toward his material is a vital source of interest; consider what would happen to these songs if the writers seemed over-enthusiastic or too sentimental. But more than tone is at stake here. In *Follow the Drinkin' Gourd* and *Woman Blue,* the folk writers' attitudes toward their material lead us to react to these writers almost as if they were characters in their own stories. In *Death Don't Have No Mercy* and *Black Is the Color,* the attitudes of the writers, in addition to making the writers into dramatic characters, also convert argument and description into powerful means for revealing feeling. Later in the book we will see that sometimes we will also have to distinguish between the writer's attitude and that of the represented speaker of the poem or lyric, especially in the case of sustained irony. Finally, we should observe that in nearly every song the writer's alter ego—the singer—has the profoundest sort of effect on the working power of the lyrics. In fact, the ambiguity and looseness that might seem to fault certain lyrics may actually be effective devices for allowing the personality of the singer to emerge as persona. This is especially true for the blues.

The last category of techniques—those centering on the audience—logically embraces, of course, all those previously discussed. But over and above the effects that the latter are intended to produce are those that come from what the audience itself brings to the work, the exact character of which is probably unpredictable by the writer. One cause of this kind of effect is *myth.* There are certain objects, characters, situations, and patterns of thought that somehow communicate with our deepest conscious-ness, stirring it into reactions which vary from individual to individual, though perhaps within a describable range. How, for example, will the reader react to *Stackerlee,* the bad-tempered gambler who challenges the devil himself?

Surely the listener, despite his moral codes, will admire
Stackerlee; but, admiration aside, who can tell exactly
what the listener will think of this villain? Stackerlee is a
mythic figure, an embodiment of total challenge to
authority, and his appeal to man's sub-rational fancy is
demonstrated in countless other figures like him in
literature and mythology. Another, less mysterious cause
of audience participation in the construction of a song or
poem is the writer's use of *suggestiveness* in general.
The poems in this section illustrate this technique better
than do the songs because poetry is fundamentally more
intellectually demanding than song. One test for sug-
gestiveness is simply to ask what the writer has stimulated
us to think about after the work is finished.

Black Is the Color

Traditional Southern Appalachian Folk Song
Sung by Joan Baez
Joan Baez in Concert, Vanguard VSD-2123

Black, black, black is the color of my true love's hair,
His lips are something wond'rous fair,
The purest eyes and the bravest hands,
I love the ground whereon he stands.

Black, black, black is the color of my true love's hair.

I love my love and well he knows,
I love the ground whereon he goes
And if my love no more I see,
My life would quickly fade away.

Black, black, black is the color of my true love's hair.

Song of Solomon

(from *The Holy Bible,* King James Version,
Chapter V, verses 10-16)

My beloved is white and ruddy,
    the chiefest among ten thousand.
His head is as the most fine gold:
    his locks are bushy, and black as a raven:
His eyes are as the eyes of doves by the rivers of waters,
    washed with milk, and fitly set:
His cheeks are as a bed of spices, as sweet flowers:
    his lips like lilies, dropping sweet smelling myrrh:
His hands are as gold rings set with the beryl:
    his belly is as bright ivory overlaid with sapphires:
His legs are as pillars of marble, set up sockets of fine gold:
    his countenance is as Lebanon, excellent as the cedars:
His mouth is most sweet: yea, he is altogether lovely.
    This is my beloved, and this my friend, O daughters of Jerusalem.

Shall I Compare Thee to a Summer's Day
William Shakespeare

Shall I compare thee to a summer's day?
Thou art more lovely and more temperate.
Rough winds do shake the darling buds of May,
And summer's lease hath all too short a date.
Sometime too hot the eye of heaven shines,
And often is his gold complexion dimmed.
And every fair from fair sometime declines,
By chance or nature's changing course untrimmed:
But thy eternal summer shall not fade,
Nor lose possession of that fair thou owest,
Nor shall Death brag thou wander'st in his shade
When in eternal lines to time thou grow'st.
   So long as men can breathe, or eyes can see,
   So long lives this, and this gives life to thee.

There Is a Garden in Her Face
Thomas Campion

There is a garden in her face,
Where roses and white lilies grow;
  A heav'nly paradise is that place,
Wherein all pleasant fruits do flow.
  There cherries grow which none may buy
  Till cherry-ripe themselves do cry.

Those cherries fairly do enclose
Of orient pearl a double row,
  Which when her lovely laughter shows,
They look like rosebuds filled with snow.
  Yet them nor peer nor prince can buy,
  Till cherry-ripe themselves do cry.

Her eyes like angels watch them still;
Her brows like bended bows do stand,
  Threat'ning with piercing frowns to kill
All that attempt with eye or hand
  Those sacred cherries to come nigh,
  Till cherry-ripe themselves do cry.

Song
Thomas Carew

Ask me no more where Jove bestows,
When June is past, the fading rose;
For in your beauty's orient deep
These flowers, as in their causes, sleep.

Ask me no more whither do stray
The golden atoms of the day;
For, in pure love, heaven did prepare
Those powders to enrich your hair.

Ask me no more whither doth haste
The nightingale, when May is past;
For in your sweet dividing throat
She winters, and keeps warm her note.

Ask me no more where those stars light
That downwards fall in dead of night;
For in your eyes they sit, and there
Fixèd become, as in their sphere.

Ask me no more if east or west
The Phoenix builds her spicy nest;
For unto you at last she flies,
And in your fragrant bosom dies.

A Celebration of Charis
Her Triumph
Ben Jonson

See the chariot at hand here of Love,
    Wherein my lady rideth!
Each that draws is a swan or a dove,
    And well the car Love guideth.
As she goes, all hearts do duty
        Unto her beauty;
And enamoured, do wish, so they might
        But enjoy such a sight,
That they still were to run by her side,
Through swords, through seas, whither she would ride.

Do but look on her eyes; they do light
    All that Love's world compriseth!
Do but look on her hair; it is bright
    As Love's star when it riseth!
Do but mark, her forehead's smoother
        Than words that soothe her!
And from her archèd brows, such a grace
        Sheds itself through the face,
As alone there triumphs to the life
All the gain, all the good of the elements' strife.

Have you seen but a bright lily grow,
    Before rude hands have touched it?
Ha' you marked but the fall o' the snow,
    Before the soil hath smutched it?
Ha' you felt the wool of bever,
        Or swan's-down ever?
Or have smelt o' the bud o' the briar,
        Or the nard in the fire?
Or have tasted the bag of the bee?
O so white! O so soft! O so sweet is she!

She Walks in Beauty

George Gordon, Lord Byron

She walks in beauty, like the night
    Of cloudless climes and starry skies;
And all that's best of dark and bright
    Meet in her aspect and her eyes:
Thus mellowed to that tender light
    Which heaven to gaudy day denies.

One shade the more, one ray the less,
    Had half impaired the nameless grace,
Which waves in every raven tress,
    Or softly lightens o'er her face;
Where thoughts serenely sweet express
    How pure, how dear their dwelling-place.

And on that cheek, and o'er that brow,
    So soft, so calm, yet eloquent,
The smiles that win, the tints that glow,
    But tell of days in goodness spent,
A mind at peace with all below,
    A heart whose love is innocent!

To Helen
Edgar Allan Poe

Helen, thy beauty is to me
   Like those Nicean barks of yore,
That gently, o'er a perfumed sea,
    The weary, way-worn wanderer bore
   To his own native shore.

On desperate seas long wont to roam,
   Thy hyacinth hair, thy classic face,
Thy Naiad airs have brought me home
   To the glory that was Greece
And the grandeur that was Rome.

Lo! in yon brilliant window-niche
   How statue-like I see thee stand!
   The agate lamp within thy hand,
Ah, Psyche, from the regions which
Are Holy Land!

A Birthday
Christina Rossetti

My heart is like a singing bird
   Whose nest is in a watered shoot:
My heart is like an apple tree
   Whose boughs are bent with thickset fruit;
My heart is like a rainbow shell
   That paddles in a halcyon sea;
My heart is gladder than all these
   Because my love is come to me.

Raise me a dais of silk and down;
   Hang it with vair and purple dyes;
Carve it in doves and pomegranates,
   And peacocks with a hundred eyes;
Work it in gold and silver grapes,
   In leaves and silver fleurs-de-lys;
Because the birthday of my life
   Is come, my love is come to me.

The Cherry Tree Carol

Traditional English Folk Ballad
Sung by Joan Baez,
Joan Baez: Volume 2, Vanguard VSD 2097

When Joseph was an old man, an old man was he,
He married Virgin Mary, The Queen of Galilee,
He married Virgin Mary, The Queen of Galilee.

Joseph and Mary walked through an orchard green,
There were berries and cherries as thick as might be seen,
There were berries and cherries as thick as might be seen.

And Mary spoke to Joseph, so meek and so mild,
"Joseph gather me some cherries, for I am with child,
Joseph gather me some cherries, for I am with child."

And Joseph flew in anger, in anger flew he,
"Let the father of the baby gather cherries for thee,
Let the father of the baby gather cherries for thee."

Then up spoke baby Jesus from in Mary's womb,
"Bend down the tallest tree that my mother might have some,
Bend down the tallest tree that my mother might have some."

And bent down the tallest branch 'til it touched Mary's hand,
Cried she, "Oh, look thou Joseph, I have cherries by command,"
Cried she, "Oh, look thou Joseph, I have cherries by command."

God's Grandeur

Gerard Manley Hopkins

The world is charged with the grandeur of God.
It will flame out, like shining from shook foil;
It gathers to a greatness, like the ooze of oil
Crushed. Why do men then now not reck his rod?

Generations have trod, have trod, have trod;
And all is seared with trade; bleared, smeared with toil;
And wears man's smudge and shares man's smell: the soil
Is bare now, nor can foot feel, being shod.

And for all this, nature is never spent;
There lives the dearest freshness deep down things;
And though the last lights off the black West went
Oh, morning, at the brown brink eastward, springs—
Because the Holy Ghost over the bent
World broods with warm breast and with ah! bright wings.

Johnny, I Hardly Knew Yeh

Traditional Irish Ballad
Sung by the Clancy Brothers,
The Clancy Brothers and Tommy Makem,
Traditional TLP 1042

Also hear Tommy Makem,
*The Clancy Brothers and Tommy Makem:
Hearty and Hellish!,* Columbia CS 8571

*When on the road to sweet Athy, haroo, haroo,
When on the road to sweet Athy, haroo, haroo,
When on the road to sweet Athy
A doleful damsel I heard cry,
"Johnny, I hardly knew yeh."*

Chorus:

*"Wi' your guns and drums and drums and guns, haroo, haroo,
"Wi' your guns and drums and drums and guns, haroo, haroo,
   "Wi your guns and drums and drums and guns
   "The enemy nearly slew yeh.
   "Oh, darlin' dear, yeh look so queer,
   "Johnny, I hardly knew yeh."*

*"Where are the eyes that looked so mild, haroo, haroo,
"Where are the eyes that looked so mild, haroo, haroo,
"Where are the eyes that looked so mild
"When my poor heart yeh first beguiled?
"Why did you skedaddle from me and the child?
"Johnny, I hardly knew yeh.*

Chorus

*"Where are the legs with which yeh run, haroo, haroo,
"Where are the legs with which yeh run, haroo, haroo,
"Where are the legs with which yeh run
"When first yeh went to carry a gun?
"Indeed your dancin' days are done.
"Johnny, I hardly knew yeh.*

Chorus

*"Yeh haven't an arm, yeh haven't a leg, haroo, haroo,
"Yeh haven't an arm, yeh haven't a leg, haroo, haroo,
"Yeh haven't an arm, yeh haven't a leg,
"You're an eyeless, boneless, chickenless egg.
"You'll have to be put with a bowl to beg.
"Johnny, I hardly knew yeh.*

Chorus

"I'm happy for to see yeh home, haroo, haroo,
"I'm happy for to see yeh home, haroo, haroo,
"I'm happy for to see yeh home
"All from the island of Ceylon—
"So low in the flesh, so high in the bone.
"Johnny, I hardly knew yeh."

   Chorus

A Hell of a Day

Tim Reynolds

This was a day of fumbling and petty accidents,
as though the population had grown all thumbs
at once. Watering her chrysanthemums,
Mrs. Kamei was surprised to see the plants
blacken, water turn to steam. Both Dote and Michiko
noted the other's absence but not her own.
Mr. Kime lifted his hat, but his head was gone.
Mr. Watanable rolled a double zero.
Photographing her son by the river bridge
Mrs. Ume pressed the shutter and overexposed her film.
Her son's yawn swallowed him. And everything turned on
when pretty Miss Mihara snapped the light switch.
Then old Mr. Ekahomo struck a match
to light his pipe, and the town caught, and dissolved in flame.

Isaiah

(from *The Holy Bible,* King James Version,
Chapter II, verses 2-4)

And it shall come to pass in the last days,
That the mountain of the Lord's house
Shall be established in the top of the mountains,
And shall be exalted above the hills;
And all nations shall flow unto it.

And many people shall go and say,
Come ye, and let us go up to the mountain of the Lord,
To the house of the God of Jacob;
And he will teach us of his ways,
And we will walk in his paths:
For out of Zion shall go forth the law,
And the word of the Lord from Jerusalem.

And he shall judge among the nations,
And shall rebuke many people:
And they shall beat their swords into plowshares,
And their spears into pruning hooks:
Nation shall not lift up sword against nation,
Neither shall they learn war any more.

Stackerlee

Traditional American Folk Song
Sung by Dave Van Ronk,
Dave Van Ronk: Folksinger, Prestige 7527

I remember one September, cold and frosty night,
Mr. Stackerlee and Billy De Lyons had a great fight.
Cryin', "When you lose your money, learn to lose."

Old Stackerlee shot six bits, Billy Lyons bet he pass,
Stackerlee out with his .45, says, "You done shot your last."
When you lose your money, learn to lose.

Well, a woman comes a-runnin', fell down on her knees,
Cryin', "Lordy Lord, Mr. Stackerlee, don't shoot my brother, please!"
When you lose your money, learn to lose.

Talk about some gambler, oughta see my Richard Lee,
He shot one thousand dollars and he come out on a three.
Cryin', "When you lose your money, learn to lose."

Well, old Stackerlee got his pistol, boy he got it fast,
Shot poor Billy through and through and it broke a lookin' glass.
Cryin', "When you lose your money, learn to lose."

Well, the deputy says to the sheriff, "You want him dead or alive?
How'n the world we gonna bring him in when he totes that .45?"
When you lose your money, learn to lose.

Old deputy leaves the office, puts his pistol on the shelf,
"You wanna go and get that badman, better do it by yourself."
When you lose your money, learn to lose.

Well, they sent for the militia, wagons come,
Loaded up with pistols and a great big Gatlin' gun.
Cryin', "When you lose your money, learn to lose."

Well, the judge says, "Mr. Stackerlee, Mr. Bad Man Stackerlee,
Gonna hang your body up and set your spirit free."
When you lose your money, learn to lose.

Well, he's standin' on his gallows, head a-way up high,
Twelve o'clock we killed him, I was glad to see him die.
Cryin', "When you lose your money, learn to lose."

Well, there's a great big rumblin' underground, "Momma what is that?"
"Ain't nothin' but old Stackerlee down in hell with his John B. Stetson hat."
Cryin', "When you lose your money, learn to lose."

Well, Stack says to the devil, "Devil, let's us have some fun,
You stab me with your pitchfork, and I'll shoot you with my gun."
When you lose your money, learn to lose.

Well, Stack says to the devil, "Put your pitchfork on the shelf,
I'm that badman they call Stackerlee. I'm gonna rule hell by myself."
When you lose your money, learn to lose.

Jonne Armestrong

Traditional English Ballad

There dwelt a man in faire Westmerland,
    Jonne Armestrong men did him call,
He had nither lands nor rents coming in,
    Yet he kept eight score men in his hall.

He had horse and harness for them all,
    Goodly steeds were all milke-white;
O the golden bands an about their necks,
    And their weapons, they were all alike.

Newes then was brought unto the king
    That there was sicke a won as hee,
That lived lyke a bold out-law,
    And robbed all the north country.

The king he writt an a letter then,
    A letter which was large and long;
He signed it with his owne hand,
    And promised to doe him no wrong.

When this letter came Jonne untill,
    His heart it was as blythe as birds on the tree:
"Never was I sent for before any king,
    My father, my grandfather, nor none but mee.

"And if wee goe the king before,
    I would we went most orderly;
Every man of you shall have his scarlet cloak,
    Laced with sillver laces three.

"Every won of you shall have his velvett coat,
    Laced with sillver lace so white;
O the golden bands an about your necks,
    Black hatts, white feathers, all alyke."

By the morrow morninge at ten of the clock,
    Towards Edenburough gon was hee,
And with him all his eight score men;
    Good lord, it was a goodly sight for to see!

When Jonne came befower the king,
    He fell downe on his knee;
"O pardon, my soveraine leige," he said,
    "O pardon my eight score men and mee!"

"Thou shalt have no pardon, thou traytor strong,
 For thy eight score men nor thee;
For to-morrow morning by ten of the clock,
 Both thou and them shall hang on the gallow-tree."

But Jonne looke'd over his left shoulder,
 Good Lord, what a grevious look looked hee!
Saying "Asking grace of a graceless face—
 Why there is none for you nor me."

But Jonne had a bright sword by his side,
 And it was made of the mettle so free,
That had not the king stept his foot aside,
 He had smitten his head from his faire bodde.

Saying, "Fight on, my merry men all,
 And see that none of you be taine;
For rather then men shall say we were hanged,
 Let them report how we were slaine."

Then, God wott, faire Eddenburrough rose,
 And so besett poore Jonne rounde,
That fowerscore and tenn of Jonnes best men
 Lay gasping all upon the ground.

Then like a mad man Jonne laide about,
 And like a mad man then fought hee,
Untill a falce Scot came Jonne behinde,
 And runn him through the faire boddee.

Saying, "Fight on, my merry men all,
 And see that none of you be taine;
And I will stand by and bleed but awhile,
 And then will I come and fight againe."

Newes then was brought to young Jonne Armestrong,
 As he stood by his nurses knee,
Who vowed if ere he lived for to be a man,
 O the treacherous Scots revengd hee'd be.

Follow the Drinkin' Gourd

Traditional Negro Folk Song
Sung by Pete Seeger,
I Can See A New Day, Columbia CS 9057
Hear also Theodore Bikel,
From Bondage to Freedom, Elektra EKS 7200

Slaves would refer to the Big Dipper as the "drinkin' gourd"
in order to deceive their masters when they sang this song.
The dipper pointed North to freedom. The old man
in the song was the contact with the underground railroad.

Chorus:

Follow the drinkin' gourd,
Follow the drinkin' gourd,
For the old man is a-waitin' for to carry you to freedom,
Follow the drinkin' gourd.

When the sun comes back, and the first quail calls,
Follow the drinkin' gourd,
When the old man is a-waitin' for to carry you to freedom,
Follow the drinkin' gourd.

Chorus

Well, the river bank will make a mighty good road,
The dead trees will show you the way,
Left foot, big foot, travelin' on,
Follow the drinkin' gourd.

Chorus

Well, the river ends between two hills,
Follow the drinkin' gourd,
There's another river on the other side,
Follow the drinkin' gourd.

Chorus

Song of Myself
Walt Whitman
(from section 33)

The disdain and calmness of martyrs,
The mother of old, condemn'd for a witch, burnt with dry
    wood, her children gazing on,
The hounded slave that flags in the race, leans by the fence,
    blowing, cover'd with sweat,
The twinges that sting like needles his legs and neck, the
    murderous buckshot and the bullets,
All these I feel or am.

I am the hounded slave, I wince at the bite of the dogs,
Hell and despair are upon me, crack and again crack the
    marksmen,
I clutch the rails of the fence, my gored ribs, thinn'd with the
    ooze of my skin,
I fall on the weeds and stones,
The riders spur their unwilling horses, haul close,
Taunt my dizzy ears and beat me violently over the head with
    whip-stocks.

Agonies are one of my changes of garments,
I do not ask the wounded person how he feels, I myself
    become the wounded person,
My hurts turn livid upon me as I lean on a cane and observe.

For My People
Margaret Walker

For my people everywhere singing their slave songs repeatedly:
their dirges and their ditties and their blues and jubilees,
praying their prayers nightly to an unknown god, bending
their knees humbly to an unseen power;

For my people lending their strength to the years: to the gone years
and the now years and the maybe years, washing ironing
cooking scrubbing sewing mending hoeing plowing digging
planting pruning patching dragging along never gaining never
reaping never knowing and never understanding;

For my playmates in the clay and dust and sand of Alabama
backyards playing baptizing and preaching, and doctor and
jail and soldier and school and mama and cooking and
playhouse and concert and store and Miss Choomby and
hair and company;

For the cramped bewildered years we went to school to learn to
know the reasons why and the answers to and the people who
and the places where and the days when, in memory of the
bitter hours when we discovered we were black and poor and
small and different and nobody wondered and nobody
understood;

For the boys and girls who grew in spite of these things to be Man
and Woman, to laugh and dance and sing and play and drink
their wine and religion and success, to marry their playmates
and bear children and then die of consumption and anemia
and lynching;

For my people thronging 47th Street in Chicago and Lenox Avenue
in New York and Rampart Street in New Orleans, lost
disinherited dispossessed and HAPPY people filling the
cabarets and taverns and other people's pockets needing
bread and shoes and milk and land and money and Something
—Something all our own;

For my people walking blindly, spreading joy, losing time being
lazy, sleeping when hungry, shouting when burdened, drinking
when hopeless, tied and shackled and tangled among ourselves
by the unseen creatures who tower over us omnisciently
and laugh;

For my people blundering and groping and floundering in the dark
of churches and schools and clubs and societies, associations
and councils and committees and conventions, distressed
and disturbed and deceived and devoured by money-hungry
glory-craving leeches, preyed on by facile force of state and
fad and novelty by false prophet and holy believer;

For my people standing staring trying to fashion a better way
from confusion from hypocrisy and misunderstanding, trying
to fashion a world that will hold all the people all the faces
all the adams and eves and their countless generations;

Let a new earth rise. Let another world be born. Let a bloody peace
be written in the sky. Let a second generation full of courage
issue forth, let a people loving freedom come to growth,
let a beauty full of healing and a strength of final clenching
be the pulse in our spirits and our blood. Let the martial songs
be written, let the dirges disappear. Let a race of men now
rise and take control!

John Henry

Traditional Negro Ballad
Hear *Sonny Terry & Brownie McGhee,*
Shouts and Blues, Fantasy 3317
Brownie McGhee and Sonny Terry Sing,
Folkways Records NYFW 2327
Big Bill Broonzy Sings Folk Songs, Folkways FA 2328

John Henry was a little baby,
Sittin' on his mammy's knee,
Said, "The Big Bend tunnel on the C. & O. road
Gonna be the death of me,
Lawd, Lawd, gonna be the death of me."

John Henry was a little baby,
Sittin' on his daddy's knee,
Point his finger at a little piece of steel,
"That's gonna be the death of me,
Lawd, Lawd, that's gonna be the death of me."

John Henry had a little woman
And her name was Mary Magdelene,
She would go to the tunnel and sing for John
Jes' to hear John Henry's hammer ring,
Lawd, Lawd, jes' to hear John Henry's hammer ring.

John Henry had a little woman
And her name was Polly Anne,
John Henry took sick and he had to go to bed,
Polly Anne drove steel like a man,
Lawd, Lawd, Polly Anne drove steel like a man.

Cap'n says to John Henry,
"Gonna bring me a steam drill 'round,
Gonna take that steam drill out on the job,
Gonna whop that steel on down,
Lawd, Lawd, gonna whop that steel on down."

John Henry told his cap'n,
Said, "A man ain't nothin' but a man,
And befo' I'd let that steam drill beat me down
I'd die with this hammer in my hand,
Lawd, Lawd, I'd die with the hammer in my hand."

Sun were hot and burnin',
Weren't no breeze atall,
Sweat ran down like water down a hill,
That day John let his hammer fall,
Lawd, Lawd, that day John let his hammer fall.

White man told John Henry,
"Nigger, damn yo' soul,
You may beat dis steam and drill of mine,—
When the rocks in the mountains turn to gold,
Lawd, Lawd, when the rocks in the mountains turn to gold."

John Henry said to his shaker,
"Shaker, why don't you sing?
I'm throwin' twelve pounds from my hips on down,
Jes' lissen to the cold steel ring,
Lawd, Lawd, jes' lissen to the cold steel ring."

O the cap'n told John Henry,
"I b'lieve this mountain's sinkin' in,"
John Henry said to his cap'n, "O my,
It's my hammer just a-hossin' in the wind,
Lawd, Lawd, it's my hammer just a-hossin' in the wind."

John Henry told his shaker,
"Shaker, you better pray,
For, if I miss this six-foot steel
Tomorrow be yo' buryin' day,
Lawd, Lawd, tomorrow be yo' buryin' day."

John Henry told his captain,
"Looky yonder what I see—
Yo' drill's done broke an' yo' hole's done choke,
An' you can't drive steel like me,
Lawd, Lawd, an' you can't drive steel like me."

John Henry was hammerin' on the mountain,
An' his hammer was strikin' fire,
He drove so hard till he broke his pore heart
An' he lied down his hammer an' he died,
Lawd, Lawd, he lied down his hammer an' he died.

They took John Henry to the graveyard
An' they buried him in the sand
An' ev'ry locomotive come roarin' by,
Says, "There lays a steel drivin' man,"
Lawd, Lawd, "There lays a steel drivin' man."

American Gothic

To Satch
(The legendary Satchell Page,
one of the star pitchers in Negro baseball)
Paul Vesey

Sometimes I feel like I will never stop
Just go on forever
Til one fine mornin'
I'm gonna reach up and grab me a handfulla stars
Swing out my long lean leg
And whip three hot strikes burnin' down the heavens
And look over at God and say
How about that!

The Man and the Machine

E. J. Pratt

By right of fires that smelted ore
Which he had tended years before,
The man whose hands were on the wheel
Could trace his kinship through her steel,
Between his body warped and bent
In every bone and ligament,
And this "eight-cylinder" stream-lined,
The finest model yet designed.
He felt his lesioned pulses strum
Against the rhythm of her hum,
And found his nerves and sinews knot
With sharper spasm as she climbed
The steeper grades, so neatly timed
From storage tank to piston shot—
This creature with the cougar grace,
This man with slag upon his face.

The Negro Mother

Langston Hughes

Children, I come back today
To tell you a story of the long dark way
That I had to climb, that I had to know
In order that the race might live and grow.
Look at my face—dark as the night—
Yet shining like the sun with love's true light.
I am the child they stole from the sand
Three hundred years ago in Africa's land.
I am the dark girl who crossed the wide sea
Carrying in my body the seed of the free.
I am the woman who worked in the field
Bringing the cotton and the corn to yield.
I am the one who labored as a slave,
Beaten and mistreated for the work that I gave—
Children sold away from me, husband sold, too.
No safety, no love, no respect was I due.
Three hundred years in the deepest South:
But God put a song and a prayer in my mouth.
God put a dream like steel in my soul.
Now, through my children, I'm reaching the goal.
Now, through my children, young and free,
I realize the blessings denied to me.
I couldn't read then. I couldn't write.
I had nothing, back there in the night.
Sometimes, the valley was filled with tears,
But I kept trudging on through the lonely years.
Sometimes, the road was hot with sun,
But I had to keep on till my work was done:
I *had* to keep on! No stopping for me—
I was the seed of the coming Free.
I nourished the dream that nothing could smother
Deep in my breast—the Negro mother.
I had only hope then, but now through you,
Dark ones of today, my dreams must come true:
All you dark children in the world out there,
Remember my sweat, my pain, my despair.
Remember my years, heavy with sorrow—
And make of those years a torch for tomorrow.
Make of my past a road to the light
Out of the darkness, the ignorance, the night.
Lift high my banner out of the dust.

Stand like free men supporting my trust.
Believe in the right, let none push you back.
Remember the whip and the slaver's track.
Remember how the strong in struggle and strife
Still bar you the way, and deny you life—
But march ever forward, breaking down bars.
Look ever upward at the sun and the stars.
Oh, my dark children, may my dreams and my prayers
Impel you forever up the great stairs—
For I will be with you till no white brother
Dares keep down the children of the Negro mother.

Woman Blue

Traditional Blues
Sung by Judy Roderick,
Woman Blue, Vanguard 79197

I know you rider, gonna miss me when I'm gone,
I know you rider, gonna miss me when I'm gone,
Miss your lovin' woman from rollin' in your arms.

Lovin' you baby is as easy as fallin' off a log,
Lovin' you baby is as easy as fallin' off a log,
I can't be your woman, baby, I'll be your dog.

I'd cut your wood and baby, I'd tend your fire,
I'd cut your wood and baby, I'd tend your fire,
I'd even haul your whiskey up from Fresno bar.

I lay down and I try to take my rest,
I lay down and I try to take my rest,
My mind it keeps ramblin' like one piece in the west.

Sun's gonna shine on my back door some day,
Sun's gonna shine on my back door some day,
Wind is gonna rise, is gonna blow my blues away.

I know you rider, gonna miss me when I'm gone,
I know you rider, gonna miss me when I'm gone,
Miss your lovin' woman from rollin' in your arms.

I Hereby Swear That to Uphold Your House

Elinor Wylie

I hereby swear that to uphold your house
I would lay my bones in quick destroying lime
Or turn my flesh to timber for all time;
Cut down my womanhood; lop off the boughs
Of that perpetual ecstasy that grows
From the heart's core; condemn it as a crime
If it be broader than a beam, or climb
Above the stature that your roof allows.
I am not the hearthstone nor the cornerstone
Within this noble fabric you have builded;
Not by my beauty was its cornice gilded;
Not on my courage were its arches thrown:
My lord, adjudge my strength, and set me where
I bear a little more than I can bear.

Death Don't Have No Mercy in This Land

Traditional Blues
Sung by Rev. Gary Davis,
Rev. Gary Davis at Newport, Vanguard 73008

Well, death don't have no mercy in this land,
Death don't have no mercy in this land,
Come to your house and he won't stay long,
You look in the bed and you'll find your mother gone.
Death don't have no mercy in this land.

He won't give you time to get ready in this land,
He won't give you time to get ready in this land,
Well, he come to your house and he won't stay long,
You look in the bed and you'll find your father gone.
He won't give you time to get ready in this land.

Well, he'll leave you standin' and cryin' in this land,
He'll leave you standin' and cryin' in this land,
He'll come to your house and he won't stay long,
You'll look in the bed and you find your sister gone.
He'll leave you standin' cryin' in this land.

Oh, death never takes a vacation in this land,
Death never takes a vacation in this land,
Well, he come to your house and he won't stay long,
You look in the bed and you find everybody gone.
Death never takes a vacation in this land.

Because I Could Not Stop for Death

Emily Dickinson

Because I could not stop for Death,
He kindly stopped for me;
The carriage held but just ourselves
And Immortality.

We slowly drove, he knew no haste,
And I had put away
My labor, and my leisure too,
For his civility.

We passed the school
    where children played
At wrestling in a ring;
We passed the fields of gazing grain,
We passed the setting sun.

We paused before a house that seemed
A swelling of the ground;
The roof was scarcely visible,
The cornice but a mound.

Since then 't is centuries; but each
Feels shorter than the day
I first surmised the horses' heads
Were toward eternity.

Fear No More the Heat o' the Sun

William Shakespeare
(from *Cymbeline,* IV, ii, 258)

Guiderius
Fear no more the heat o' the sun,
    Nor the furious winter's rages;
Thou thy worldly task hast done,
    Home art gone, and ta'en thy wages:
Golden lads and girls all must,
As chimney-sweepers, come to dust.

Arviragus
Fear no more the frown o' the great;
    Thou art past the tyrant's stroke;
Care no more to clothe and eat;
    To thee the reed is as the oak:
The scepter, learning, physic, must
All follow this, and come to dust.

Guiderius
Fear no more the lightning-flash,

Arviragus
    Nor the all-dreaded thunder-stone;

Guiderius
Fear not slander, censure rash;

Arviragus
    Thou hast finished joy and moan:

Both
All lovers young, all lovers must
Consign to thee, and come to dust.

Guiderius
No exorciser harm thee!

Arviragus
Nor no witchcraft charm thee!

Guiderius
Ghost unlaid forbear thee!

Arviragus
Nothing ill come near thee!

Both
Quiet consummation have;
And renownèd be thy grave!

Death, Be Not Proud

John Donne

Death, be not proud, though some have called thee
Mighty and dreadful, for thou art not so;
For those whom thou think'st thou dost overthrow
Die not, poor Death; nor yet canst thou kill me.
From rest and sleep, which but thy pictures be,
Much pleasure; then from thee much more must flow;
And soonest our best men with thee do go—
Rest of their bones and souls' delivery!
Thou'rt slave to fate, chance, kings, and desperate men,
And dost with poison, war, and sickness dwell;
And poppy or charms can make us sleep as well
And better than thy stroke. Why swell'st thou then?
One short sleep past, we wake eternally,
And Death shall be no more: Death, thou shalt die.

Would You Trade Your Pain

John Bruce

Would you trade your pain
For a part of my death?
If brothers were gentler than this
Would they feed us their share of the light?

Has all death got this wet mouth
And dry skin as though washed
Over and over and towelled
Just too clean as plaster?

Oh, Jesus, yes, it's pure like that
And afterwards the sound of it
Is like the colour of ashes
Rubbed between the palms.

Do Not Go Gentle into That Good Night
Dylan Thomas

Do not go gentle into that good night,
Old age should burn and rave at close of day;
Rage, rage against the dying of the light.

Though wise men at their end know dark is right,
Because their words have forked no lightning they
Do not go gentle into that good night.

Good men, the last wave by, crying how bright
Their frail deeds might have danced in a green bay,
Rage, rage against the dying of the light.

Wild men who caught and sang the sun in flight,
And learn, too late, they grieved it on its way,
Do not go gentle into that good night.

Grave men, near death, who see with blinding sight
Blind eyes could blaze like meteors and be gay,
Rage, rage against the dying of the light.

And you, my father, there on the sad height,
Curse, bless, me now with your fierce tears, I pray
Do not go gentle into that good night.
Rage, rage against the dying of the light.

2

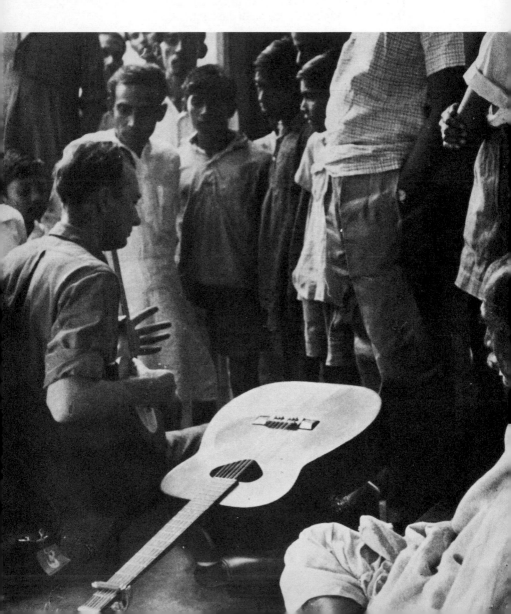

Pete Seeger

In the last decade, England and North America witnessed an astonishing development of what we have termed "authentic" popular song. As we pointed out in the General Introduction, songs that are "authentic" try to do justice to ordinary life. They "tell it like it is" in poetry of protest, social comment, and realistic love. They also tell it like their composers want it to be. In doing so, however, these songs do not become merely escapist, for the wishes they express reflect a quest for integrity and honesty. A writer of authentic song may be romantic and idealistic, but we sense that his compositions are true to what is original both in him and his audience. "Inauthentic" songs are written for people who are afraid of life and who would rather conform than think and feel for themselves.

One reason for the present flowering of authentic popular song was the foundation laid down by the contemporary folk song movement. Inspired by men like Pete Seeger, Woody Guthrie, and Huddie Ledbetter in the United States, and Ewan MacColl in Great Britain, a small, unrecognized group of white and black performers had been writing and playing folk style ballads about modern life ever since the Great Depression. These ballads championed the common man and the oppressed, and spoke of things that commercial pop song carefully avoided. When the young generation of the 60's sought to develop the honesty and realism they discovered in "rhythm and blues," they found this rich tradition of "people's" songs waiting for them.

In this section we consider the work of Pete Seeger, the leading perpetuator of that tradition. To appreciate Seeger's art properly, it is unwise to consider his lyrics as only lyrics, or his music only as music, or even his songs only as songs. Rather, we must imagine hearing and seeing Seeger singing his songs to a specific audience, a performance in which typically a hall full of strangers has shrunk into a large living room where the strangers suddenly feel like neighbors and each individual becomes intensely aware of his relation to a community.

Then we can perceive the true aesthetic functions of Seeger's poetry and music—the absolutely simple statements of emotion and belief moving through individual differences (but still respecting them) and welding men, women, and children into a public consciousness; the sketches of human struggle that bring into the "living room" he creates people of all nations and times; and the hootenanny music that invites his audience to lift their voices in an immediate union of song.

Not only Seeger, but also showmen, gospel singers, and folk bards throughout the ages demonstrate how important audience-involvement can be. Poets, too, may work in this rhetorical dimension. Associated with Seeger's songs in this section are poems by Walt Whitman, Percy Shelley, and William Blake that also require us to reconstruct a public and an actual performer or speaker before they can be fully appreciated. When we make that imaginative effort, however, we will find that these poets are not merely propagandists. For them, as for Seeger, the thoroughly democratic philosophy they express belongs to the essence of popular art, which is of and for the people.

My Father's Mansions

Words and Music by Pete Seeger
Waist Deep in the Big Muddy and Other Love Songs,
Columbia CS 9505

My father's mansion has many rooms
With room for all of His children
As long as we do share His love
And see that all are free.

And see that all are free to grow
And see that all are free to know
And free to open or to close
The door of their own room.

What is a room without a door
Which sometimes locks or stands ajar?
What is a room without a wall
To keep out sight and sound from all?

And dwellers in each room should have
The right to choose their own design
And color schemes to suit their own
Though differing from mine.

My father's mansion's many rooms
Have room for all of His children
If we do but share in His love
And see that all are free.

The choice is ours to share this earth
With all its many joys abound
Or to continue as we have
And burn God's mansion down.

My father's mansion's many rooms
Have room for all of His children
If we do but share in His love
And see that all are free.

Thou Mother with Thy Equal Brood

Walt Whitman
(from sections 1, 5, and 6)

Thou Mother with thy equal brood,
Thou varied chain of different States, yet one identity only,
A special song before I go I'd sing o'er all the rest,
For thee, the future.

I'd sow a seed for thee of endless Nationality,
I'd fashion thy ensemble including body and soul,
I'd show away ahead thy real Union, and how it may be
        accomplish'd.

The paths to the house I seek to make,
But leave to those to come the house itself.

Belief I sing, and preparation;
As Life and Nature are not great with reference to the present only,
But greater still from what is yet to come,
Out of that formula for thee I sing.

          *   *   *

Thee in thy future,
Thee in thy only permanent life, career, thy own unloosen'd mind,
        thy soaring spirit,
Thee as another equally needed sun, radiant, ablaze, swift-moving,
        fructifying all,
Thee risen in potent cheerfulness and joy, in endless great hilarity,
Scattering for good the cloud that hung so long, that weigh'd so
        long upon the mind of man,
The doubt, suspicion, dread, of gradual, certain decadence
        of man;
Thee in thy larger, saner brood of female, male—thee in thy
        athletes, moral, spiritual, South, North, West, East,
(To thy immortal breasts, Mother of All, thy every daughter, son,
        endear'd alike, forever equal,)
Thee in thy own musicians, singers, artists, unborn yet, but certain,
Thee in thy moral wealth and civilization, (until which thy proudest
        material civilization must remain in vain,)
Thee in thy all-supplying, all-enclosing worship—thee in no single
        bible, saviour, merely,
Thy saviours countless, latent within thyself, thy bibles incessant
        within thyself, equal to any, divine as any,
(Thy soaring course thee formulating, not in thy two great wars,
        nor in thy century's visible growth,
But far more in these leaves and chants, thy chants, great Mother!)

Thee in an education grown of thee, in teachers, studies, students,
    born of thee,
Thee in thy democratic fêtes en-masse, thy high original festivals,
    operas, lecturers, preachers,
Thee in thy ultimata, (the preparations only now completed,
    the edifice on sure foundations tied,)
Thee in thy pinnacles, intellect, thought, thy topmost rational joys,
    thy love and godlike aspiration,
In thy resplendent coming literati, thy full-lung'd orators, thy
    sacerdotal bards, kosmic savans,
These! these in thee, (certain to come,) to-day I prophesy.

Land tolerating all, accepting all, not for the good alone, all good
    for thee,
Land in the realms of God to be a realm unto thyself,
Under the rule of God to be a rule unto thyself.
(Lo, where arise three peerless stars,
To be thy natal stars my country, Ensemble, Evolution, Freedom,
Set in the sky of Law.)

Land of unprecedented faith, God's faith,
Thy soil, thy very subsoil, all upheav'd,
The general inner earth so long so sedulously draped over, now
    hence for what it is boldly laid bare,
Open'd by thee to heaven's light for benefit of bale.
Not for success alone,
Not to fair-sail unintermitted always,
The storm shall dash thy face, the murk of war and worse than war
    shall cover thee all over,
(Wert capable of war, its tugs and trials? be capable of peace,
    its trials,
For the tug and mortal strain of nations come at last in prosperous
    peace, not war;)
In many a smiling mask death shall approach beguiling thee, thou
    in disease shalt swelter,
The livid cancer spread its hideous claws, clinging upon thy
    breasts, seeking to strike thee deep within,
Consumption of the worst, moral consumption, shall rouge thy face
    with hectic,
But thou shalt face thy fortunes, thy diseases, and surmount
    them all,
Whatever they are to-day and whatever through time they may be,
They each and all shall lift and pass away and cease from thee,

While thou, Time's spirals rounding, out of thyself, thyself still
    extricating, fusing,
Equable, natural, mystical Union thou, (the mortal with immortal
    blent,)
Shalt soar toward the fulfilment of the future, the spirit of the body
    and the mind,
The soul, its destinies.

The soul, its destinies, the real real,
(Purport of all these apparitions of the real;)
In thee America, the soul, its destinies,
Thou globe of globes! thou wonder nebulous!
But many a throe of heat and cold convuls'd, (by these thyself
    solidifying,)
Thou mental, moral orb—thou New, indeed new, Spiritual World!
The Present holds thee not—for such vast growth as thine,
For such unparallel'd flight as thine, such brood as thine,
The Future only holds thee and can hold thee.

Oh, Had I a Golden Thread

Words and Music by Pete Seeger
Rainbow Quest, Folkways FA 24543

Oh, had I a golden thread
And needle so fine,
I'd weave a magic strand
Of rainbow design—
Of rainbow design.

In it I would weave the bravery
Of women giving birth,
In it I would weave the innocence
Of children over all the earth—
Children of all earth.

Far over the water,
I'd reach my magic band,
To every city
Through every single land—
Through every land.

Show my brothers and my sisters
My rainbow design,
Bind up this sorry world
With hand and heart and mind—
Hand and heart and mind.

Far over the waters,
I'd reach my magic band
To every human being
So they would understand—
So they'd understand.

Oh, if I had a golden thread
And needle so fine,
I'd weave a magic strand
Of rainbow design—
Of rainbow design.

I Give You the End of a Golden String

William Blake

I give you the end of a golden string;
    Only wind it into a ball,
It will lead you in at Heaven's gate,
    Built in Jerusalem's wall.

Talking Union

Pete Seeger
Talking Union, Folkways 5285

If you want higher wages let me tell you what to do,
You got to talk to the workers in the shop with you.
You got to build you a union, got to build it strong,
But if you all stick together, boys, 'twon't be long.
You get shorter hours . . . better working conditions . . .
Vacations with pay . . . take the kids to the seashore.

It ain't quite this simple, so I'd better explain
Just why you got to ride on the union train,
'Cause if you wait for the boss to raise your pay,
We'll be waitin' till judgment day.
We'll all be buried . . . gone to heaven . . .
St. Peter'll be the straw boss then, boys.

Now, you know you're underpaid but the boss says you ain't,
He speeds up the work till you're about to faint.
You may be down and out but you ain't beaten,
You can pass out a leaflet and call a meetin',
Talk it over . . . speak your mind . . .
Decide to do something about it.

Course, the boss may persuade some poor damn' fool
To go to your meeting and act like a stool;
But you can always tell a stool, though, that's a fact;
He's got a rotten streak running down his back.
He doesn't have to stool . . .
He'll always get along . . .
On what he takes out of blind men's cups.

You got a union now and you're sitting pretty,
Put some of the boys on the steering committee.
The boss won't listen when one guy squawks,
But he's got to listen when the union talks . . .
He'd better . . . Be mighty lonely . . .
Everybody decided to walk out on him.

Suppose they're working you so hard it's just outrageous,
And they're paying you all starvation wages,
You go to the boss, and the boss will yell,
"Before I raise your pay I'd see you all in hell."
Well, he's puffing a big cigar and feeling mighty slick,
'Cause he thinks he's got your union licked.
He looks out the window and what does he see
But a thousand pickets, and they all agree
He's a bastard . . . unfair . . . slavedriver.
. . . Bet he beats his own wife.

Now, boys, you've come to the hardest time;
The boss will try to bust your picket line;
He'll call out the police and the National Guard,
They'll tell you it's a crime to have a union card.
They'll raid your meetings and hit you on the head,
They'll call every one of you a goddam red
Unpatriotic . . . Moscow agents . . .
Bomb throwers . . . even the kids.

But out in Detroit here's what they found,
And out in Frisco here's what they found,
And out in Pittsburgh here's what they found,
And down at Bethlehem here's what they found—
That if you don't let redbaiting break you up,
And if you don't let stool pigeons break you up,
And if you don't let vigilantes break you up,
And if you don't let race hatred break you up,
You'll win . . . what I mean, take it easy—but take it.

Original Talking Blues

Traditional American
This is the basis of Pete Seeger's *Talking Union*
and scores of other satirical and nonsensical "talking blues"
songs. They are spoken and played in the same manner.

1

If you want to go to heaven let me tell you what to do,
You gotta grease your feet in a little mutton stew,
Slide out of the devil's hand and ooze over to the Promised Land.
    Take it easy, boy, but go greasy.

2

I was down in the holler just a-settin' on a log,
My finger on the trigger and my eye on a hog;
I pulled that trigger and the gun went "zip,"
And I grabbed that hog with all of my grip.
    Course I can't eat hog eyes, but I love chitlins.

3

Mama's in the kitchen fixin' the yeast,
Poppa's in the bedroom greasin' his feet,
Sister's in the cellar squeezin' up the hops,
Brother's at the window just a-watchin' for the cops.
    Drinkin' home-brew—makes you happy.

4

Down in the hen house on my knees,
I thought I heard a chicken sneeze,
But it was only the rooster sayin' his prayers,
Thankin' the Lord for the hens upstairs.
    Rooster prayin', hens a-layin'. Little pullets
        just pluggin' away best they know how.

5

Now I'm just a city dude a-livin' out of town,
Everybody knows me as Moonshine Brown;
I make the beer, and I drink the slop,
Got nine little orphans that calls me Pop.
    I'm patriotic—raisin' soldiers, Red Cross nurses.

6

Ain't no use me workin' so hard,
I got a gal in the rich folk's yard,
They kill a chicken, she sends me the head;
She thinks I'm workin, I'm a-layin' up in bed.
    Just dreamin' about her. Havin' a good time . . . two other women . . .

'Butch' Weldy

Edgar Lee Masters

After I got religion and steadied down
They gave me a job in the canning works,
And every morning I had to fill
The tank in the yard with gasoline,
That fed the blow-fires in the sheds
To heat the soldering irons.
And I mounted a rickety ladder to do it,
Carrying buckets full of the stuff.
One morning, as I stood there pouring,
The air grew still and seemed to heave,
And I shot up as the tank exploded,
And down I came with both legs broken,
And my eyes burned crisp as a couple of eggs.
For someone left a blow-fire going,
And something sucked the flame in the tank.
The Circuit Judge said whoever did it
Was a fellow-servant of mine, and so
Old Rhodes' son didn't have to pay me.
And I sat on the witness stand as blind
As Jack the Fiddler, saying over and over,
'I didn't know him at all.'

Song to the Men of England

Percy Bysshe Shelley

I
Men of England, wherefore plough
For the lords who lay ye low?
Wherefore weave with toil and care
The rich robes your tyrants wear?
II
Wherefore feed, and clothe, and save,
From the cradle to the grave,
Those ungrateful drones who would
Drain your sweat—nay, drink your blood?
III
Wherefore, Bees of England, forge
Many a weapon, chain, and scourge,
That these stingless drones may spoil
The forced produce of your toil?
IV
Have ye leisure, comfort, calm,
Shelter, food, love's gentle balm?
Or what is it ye buy so dear
With your pain and with your fear?
V
The seed ye sow, another reaps;
The wealth ye find, another keeps;
The robes ye weave, another wears;
The arms ye forge, another bears.
VI
Sow seed,—but let no tyrant reap;
Find wealth,—let no impostor heap;
Weave robes,—let not the idle wear;
Forge arms,—in your defence to bear.
VII
Shrink to your cellars, holes, and cells;
In halls ye deck another dwells.
Why shake the chains ye wrought? Ye see
The steel ye tempered glance on ye.
VIII
With plough and spade, and hoe and loom,
Trace your grave, and build your tomb,
And weave your winding-sheet, till fair
England be your sepulchre.

The New Jerusalem

William Blake

And did those feet in ancient time
Walk upon England's mountains green?
And was the holy Lamb of God
On England's pleasant pastures seen?

And did the Countenance Divine
Shine forth upon our clouded hills?
And was Jerusalem builded here
Among these dark Satanic Mills?

Bring me my Bow of burning gold:
Bring me my Arrows of desire:
Bring me my Spear: O clouds unfold!
Bring me my Chariot of fire.

I will not cease from Mental Fight,
Nor shall my Sword sleep in my hand
Till we have built Jerusalem
In England's green & pleasant Land.

The Big Muddy

Words and Music by Pete Seeger
Waist Deep in the Big Muddy
and Other Love Songs, Columbia CS 9505

It was back in nineteen forty-two,
I was part of a good platoon;
We were on maneuvers in a-Loozianna,
One night by the light of the moon;
The captain told us to ford a river,
And that's how it all begun.
We were knee deep in the Big Muddy
But the big fool said to move on.

The sergeant said, "Sir, are you sure,
This is the best way back to the base?"
"Sergeant, go on; I once forded this river
Just a mile above this place;
It'll be a little soggy but just keep slogging,
We'll soon be on dry ground."
We were waist deep in the Big Muddy
And the big fool said to push on.

The sergeant said, "With all this equipment
No man'll be able to swim";
"Sergeant, don't be a nervous nellie,"
The Captain said to him;
"All we need is a little determination;
Men, follow me, I'll lead on."
We were neck deep in the Big Muddy
And the big fool said to push on.

All of a sudden, the moon clouded over,
We heard a gurgling cry;
A few seconds later, the captain's helmet
Was all that floated by;
The sergeant said, "Turn around men,
I'm in charge from now on."
And we just made it out of the Big Muddy
With the captain dead and gone.

We stripped and dived and found his body
Stuck in the old quicksand;
I guess he didn't know that the water was deeper
Than the place he'd once before been;
Another stream had joined the Big Muddy
Just a half mile from where we'd gone.
We'd been lucky to escape from the Big Muddy
When the damn fool said to push on.

Well, maybe you'd rather not draw any moral,
I'll leave that to yourself;
Maybe you're still walking and you're still talking
And you'd like to keep your health;
But every time I read the papers
That old feeling comes on:
Waist deep in the Big Muddy
And the big fool says to push on.

Waist deep in the Big Muddy
And the Big Fool says to push on;
Waist deep in the Big Muddy
And the Big Fool says to push on;
Waist deep! Neck deep! Soon even a tall
Man'll be over his head!
Waist deep in the Big Muddy
And the Big Fool says to push on!

The Shield of Achilles

W. H. Auden

She looked over his shoulder
   For vines and olive trees,
Marble, well-governed cities
   And ships upon wine-dark seas;
But there on the shining metal
   His hands had put instead
An artificial wilderness
   And a sky like lead.

A plain without a feature, bare and brown,
   No blade of grass, no sign of neighborhood,
Nothing to eat and nowhere to sit down;
   Yet, congregated on that blankness, stood
   An unintelligible multitude,
A million eyes, a million boots, in line,
Without expression, waiting for a sign.

Out of the air a voice without a face
   Proved by statistics that some cause was just
In tones as dry and level as the place;
   No one was cheered and nothing was discussed,
   Column by column, in a cloud of dust,
They marched away, enduring a belief
Whose logic brought them, somewhere else, to grief.

She looked over his shoulder
   For ritual pieties,
White flower-garlanded heifers,
   Libation and sacrifice:
But there on the shining metal
   Where the altar should have been
She saw by his flickering forge-light
   Quite another scene.

Barbed wire enclosed an arbitrary spot
   Where bored officials lounged (one cracked a joke)
And sentries sweated for the day was hot;
   A crowd of ordinary decent folk
   Watched from outside and neither moved nor spoke
As three pale figures were led forth and bound
To three posts driven upright in the ground.

The mass and majesty of this world, all
    That carries weight and always weighs the same,
Lay in the hands of others; they were small
    And could not hope for help, and no help came;
    What their foes liked to do was done; their shame
Was all the worst could wish: they lost their pride
And died as men before their bodies died.

        She looked over his shoulder
          For athletes at their games,
        Men and women in a dance
          Moving their sweet limbs,
        Quick, quick, to music;
          But there on the shining shield
        His hands had set no dancing-floor
          But a weed-choked field.

A ragged urchin, aimless and alone,
    Loitered about that vacancy; a bird
Flew up to safety from his well-aimed stone:
    That girls are raped, that two boys knife a third,
    Were axioms to him, who'd never heard
Of any world where promises were kept
Or one could weep because another wept.

        The thin-lipped armorer
          Hephaestos hobbled away;
        Thetis of the shining breasts
          Cried out in dismay
        At what the God had wrought
          To please her son, the strong
        Iron-hearted man-slaying Achilles
          Who would not live long.

Who Knows?

Words and Music by Pete Seeger
Young vs. Old, Columbia CS 9873

I wish this loving would never end.
But when at last we go to sleep,
Who knows, who knows?
Some day, some night, we'll meet again.

I wish this summer would never end.
But when at last I got to go back to town,
Who knows, who knows?
Someday we'll have another season in the sun.

I wish this life would never end.
But when at last I got to go,
Who knows, who knows?
I think my human race will carry on.

I wish this race of ours would never end.
But when at last we join the dinosaurs,
Who knows, who knows?
I think the good green earth will keep a-rolling on!

I wish this good green earth would never end.
But when at last it burns or freezes cold,
Who knows, who knows?
I think our sparkling galaxy will keep a-glowing on!

I wish this milky way of stars would never end.
But when at last it shrinks once more,
Who knows, who knows?
Someday it may explode anew.

I wish this loving world would never end.
But when at last we go to sleep,
Who knows, who knows?
Some day, some night, we'll meet again!

Then who knows, who knows?
Our star might glow again.
Who knows, who knows?
Our earth might form again.
Who knows, who knows?
It might turn green again.
Who knows, who knows?
Our race might rise again.
Who knows, who knows?
You and I might meet again.

Since Brass, nor Stone, nor Earth
William Shakespeare

Since brass, nor stone, nor earth, nor boundless sea,
But sad mortality o'er-sways their power,
How with this rage shall beauty hold a plea,
Whose action is no stronger than a flower?
O, how shall summer's honey breath hold out
Against the wrackful siege of battering days,
When rocks impregnable are not so stout,
Nor gates of steel so strong, but Time decays?
O fearful meditation! where, alack,
Shall Time's best jewel from Time's chest lie hid?
Or what strong hand can hold his swift foot back?
Or who his spoil of beauty can forbid?
   O, none, unless this miracle have might,
   That in black ink my love may still shine bright.

To His Coy Mistress

Andrew Marvell

Had we but world enough, and time,
This coyness, Lady, were no crime.
We would sit down, and think which way
To walk, and pass our long love's day.
Thou by the Indian Ganges' side
Shouldst rubies find; I by the tide
Of Humber would complain. I would
Love you ten years before the Flood;
And you should, if you please, refuse
Till the conversion of the Jews.
My vegetable love should grow
Vaster than empires, and more slow.
An hundred years should go to praise
Thine eyes, and on thy forehead gaze;
Two hundred to adore each breast;
But thirty thousand to the rest:
An age, at least, to every part,
And the last age should show your heart.
For, Lady, you deserve this state;
Nor would I love at lower rate.
    But, at my back, I always hear
Time's winged chariot hurrying near:
And yonder, all before us lie
Deserts of vast eternity.
Thy beauty shall no more be found;
Nor, in the marble vault, shall sound
My echoing song. Then worms shall try
That long preserved virginity:
And your quaint honour turn to dust;
And into ashes all my lust.
The grave's a fine and private place,
But none, I think, do there embrace.

    Now, therefore, while the youthful hue
Sits on thy skin like morning dew,
And while thy willing soul transpires
At every pore with instant fires,
Now let us sport us while we may;
And now, like amorous birds of prey,
Rather at once our time devour,
Than languish in his slow-chapt power.
Let us roll all our strength, and all
Our sweetness, up into one ball;
And tear our pleasures, with rough strife,
Thorough the iron gates of life.
    Thus, though we cannot make our sun
Stand still, yet we will make him run.

3

Tim Buckley

Turning to the songs of Tim Buckley, we again need to consider performance and audience involvement as well as the songs themselves. In fact, this three-way approach is normally required in order to appreciate any popular song. In Buckley's case, however, lyrics and music are more self-sustaining than they are in Pete Seeger's work, and further the audience involvement itself is of a very different character. Buckley's songs incorporate the beliefs and experiences of sensitive, young North Americans as individuals, not as members of a people or a community.

Buckley's work is primarily *lyrical,* as it is mainly an expression of personal feeling and conviction; but indirectly it is also frequently *public* or *rhetorical,* as the feelings and beliefs expressed are immediately shared by his particular audience. We shall call this audience the "New Generation," not only because they are young but because they seek a new generation of life in this world. The New Generation does not include the larger number of young people who are uninterested in such a renewal. Buckley and the other leading young songwriters of today may wish to win over these more passive youths, but their songs are shaped by those who want change.

How then might we characterize the perspective of the young songwriters and their followers who constitute the New Generation? We suggest that to wear the spectacles of the New Generation is to look through glasses of wonder. As we indicated in the General Introduction, in a state of wonder we perceive people and things as they are in themselves, without calculating how we can use them. We also play with them, so to speak, so that both they and we can have a more luminous existence. And always in wonder we seek surprising unity and the discovery of beautiful potentials in what is given to us.

This is an aesthetic outlook, but it also has profound implications for ethics. For, how must the modern world appear to one who takes the aesthetic perspective? Are people free to be what they are, or must they shrink themselves into mere things that fit neatly and efficiently into an incredibly complex, non-human technology? Are there at least some objects that are appreciated for their own sakes, or does society and the demands it makes on us tend to turn everything into goods and services, status symbols and dollar values? And what about play? Is there anything natural, child-like, or joyous in our desperate search for amusement and escape? Asking these questions, we can share the viewpoint of the New Generation and its poet-singers and understand not only their anger with the world that seeks to possess them, but also their confidence in their ability to resist. The aesthetic, existentialist perspective they adopt is backed by powerful organic forces which once released are not likely to be stopped up again.

One very beautiful song by Buckley, *Goodbye and Hello,* reflects all that we have been saying here and should be carefully studied as a comprehensive expression of New Generation thinking. We present it, however, in association with poems written from perspectives that sometimes differ widely from the one it expresses. Our reason for doing so is at once technical and humanistic: we believe that it is in the interest both of the beginning writer and the student as a human being to develop empathy, the ability to see life as others see it. Through empathy one vastly increases his possibilities for making choices both in art and life. Empathy also leads to increasing tolerance, but this tolerance need not result in surrender to pure relativism. Spectacles can be weak and distorting as well as merely different, and when they are, the man who wears them will find both his life and work impaired. We can never be sure about spectacles, however, until we try to look through them ourselves—at least in our imagination.

In arranging these poems for comparison with *Goodbye and Hello,* we have focused on five aspects of the song which significantly reflect the New Generation perspective and which the poems illuminate by way of contrast or similarity: world outlook, perspective of the child, attitude toward the body, attitude toward country, and perspective of the puritan.

Finally, we should qualify our account of Buckley's work by pointing out that sometimes Buckley is purely lyrical. *Morning-Glory* and *Once I Was* do not require us to take the perspective of any special audience before they can work on us; all we need for these songs is sensitivity.

Goodbye and Hello

Music and Words by Tim Buckley
Goodbye and Hello, Electra EKS 7318

The antique people are down in the dungeons
  Run by machines and afraid of the tax
Their heads in the grave and their hands on their eyes
  Hauling their hearts around circular tracks
Pretending forever their masquerade towers
  Are not really riddled with widening cracks
    And I wave goodbye to iron
    And smile hello to the air

O the new children dance	*I am young*
All around the balloons	*I will live*
Swaying by chance	*I am strong*
To the breeze from the moon	*I can give*
Painting the sky	*You the strange*
With the colors of sun	*Seed of day*
Freely they fly	*Feel the change*
As all become one	*Know the Way*

The velocity addicts explode on the highways
  Ignoring the journey and moving so fast
Their nerves fall apart and they gasp but can't breathe
  They run from the cops of the skeleton past
Petrified by tradition in a nightmare they stagger
  Into nowhere at all and then look up aghast
    And I wave goodbye to speed
    And smile hello to a rose

O the new children play	*I am young*
Under juniper trees	*I will live*
Sky blue or grey	*I am strong*
They continue at ease	*I can give*
Moving so slow	*You the strange*
That serenely they can	*Seed of day*
Gracefully grow	*Feel the change*
And yes still understand	*Know the Way*

The king and the queen in their castle of billboards
  Sleepwalk down the hallways dragging behind
All their possessions and transient treasures
  As they go to worship the electronic shrine
On which is playing the late late commercial
  In that hollowest house of the opulent blind
    And I wave goodbye to Mammon
    And smile hello to a stream

O the new children buy	I am young
All the world for a song	I will live
Without a dime	I am strong
To which they belong	I can give
Nobody owns	You the strange
Anything anywhere	Seed of day
Everyone's grown	Feel the change
Up so big they can share	Know the Way

The vaudeville generals cavort on the stage
  And shatter their audience with submachine guns
And Freedom and Violence the acrobat clowns
  Do a balancing act on the graves of our sons
While the tapdancing Emperor sings "War is peace"
  And Love the Magician disappears in the fun
    And I wave goodbye to murder
    And smile hello to the rain

O the new children can't	I am young
Tell a foe from a friend	I will live
Quick to enchant	I am strong
And so glad to extend	I can give
Handfuls of dawn	You the strange
To kaleidoscope men	Seed of day
Come from beyond	Feel the change
The Great Wall of Skin	Know the Way

The bloodless husbands are jesters who listen
Like sheep to the shrieks and commands of their wives
And the men who aren't men leave the women alone
See them all faking love on a bed made of knives
Afraid to discover or trust in their bodies
And in secret divorce they will never survive
And I wave goodbye to ashes
And smile hello to a girl

O the new children kiss   *I am young*
They are so proud to learn   *I will live*
Womanhood bliss   *I am strong*
And the manfire that burns   *I can give*
Knowing no fear   *You the strange*
They take off their clothes   *Seed of day*
Honest and clear   *Feel the change*
As a river that flows   *Know the Way*

The antique people are fading out slowly
Like newspapers flaming in mind suicide
Godless and sexless directionless loons
Their sham sandcastles dissolve in the tide
They put on their deathmasks and compromise daily
The new children will live for the elders have died
And I wave goodbye to America
And smile hello to the world

World Outlook

The World
Henry Vaughan

I saw Eternity the other night,
Like a great ring of pure and endless light,
    All calm, as it was bright;
And round beneath it, Time in hours, days, years,
    Driven by the spheres
Like a vast shadow moved; in which the world
    And all her train were hurled.
The doting lover in his quaintest strain
    Did there complain;
Near him, his lute, his fancy, and his flights,
    Wit's sour delights;
With gloves, and knots, the silly snares of pleasure,
    Yet his dear treasure,
All scattered lay, while he his eyes did pour
    Upon a flower.

The darksome statesman, hung with weights and woe,
Like a thick midnight-fog, moved there so slow,
    He did not stay, nor go;
Condemning thoughts—like sad eclipses—scowl
    Upon his soul,
And clouds of crying witnesses without
    Pursued him with one shout.
Yet digged the mole, and lest his ways be found,
    Worked underground,
Where he did clutch his prey; but one did see
    That policy.
Churches and altars fed him; perjuries
    Were gnats and flies;
It rained about him blood and tears, but he
    Drank them as free.

The fearful miser on a heap of rust
Sat pining all his life there, did scarce trust
 His own hands with the dust,
Yet would not place one piece above, but lives
 In fear of thieves.
Thousands there were as frantic as himself,
 And hugged each one his pelf;
The downright epicure placed heav'n in sense,
 And scorned pretence;
While others, slipped into a wide excess,
 Said little less;
The weaker sort slight, trivial wares enslave,
 Who think them brave;
And poor, despisèd Truth sat counting by
 Their victory.

Yet some, who all this while did weep and sing,
And sing and weep, soared up into the ring;
 But most would use no wing.
Oh, fools—said I—thus to prefer dark night
 Before true light!
To live in grots and caves, and hate the day
 Because it shows the way;
The way, which from this dead and dark abode
 Leads up to God;
A way where you might tread the sun, and be
 More bright than he!
But as I did their madness so discuss,
 One whispered thus,
'This ring the Bridegroom did for none provide,
 But for His bride.'

I Am Waiting
Lawrence Ferlinghetti

I am waiting for my case to come up
and I am waiting
for a rebirth of wonder
and I am waiting for someone
to really discover America
and wail
and I am waiting
for the discovery
of a new symbolic western frontier
and I am waiting
for the American Eagle
to really spread its wings
and straighten up and fly right
and I am waiting
for the Age of Anxiety
to drop dead
and I am waiting
for the war to be fought
which will make the world safe
for anarchy
and I am waiting
for the final withering away
of all governments
and I am perpetually awaiting
a rebirth of wonder

I am waiting for the Second Coming
and I am waiting
for a religious revival
to sweep thru the state of Arizona
and I am waiting
for the Grapes of Wrath to be stored
and I am waiting
for them to prove
that God is really American
and I am seriously waiting
for Billy Graham and Elvis Presley
to exchange roles seriously
and I am waiting
to see God on television
piped onto church altars

if only they can find
the right channel
to tune in on
and I am waiting
for the Last Supper to be served again
with a strange new appetizer
and I am perpetually awaiting
a rebirth of wonder

I am waiting for my number to be called
and I am waiting
for the living end
and I am waiting
for dad to come home
his pockets full
of irradiated silver dollars
and I am waiting
for the atomic tests to end
and I am waiting happily
for things to get much worse
before they improve
and I am waiting
for the Salvation Army to take over
and I am waiting
for the human crowd
to wander off a cliff somewhere
clutching its atomic umbrella
and I am waiting
for Ike to act
and I am waiting
for the meek to be blessed
and inherit the earth
without taxes
and I am waiting
for forests and animals
to reclaim the earth as theirs
and I am waiting
for a way to be devised
to destroy all nationalisms
without killing anybody
and I am waiting
for linnets and planets to fall like rain
and I am waiting for lovers and weepers
to lie down together again
in a new rebirth of wonder

I am waiting for the Great Divide to be crossed
and I am anxiously waiting
for the secret of eternal life to be discovered
by an obscure general practitioner
and save me forever from certain death
and I am waiting
for life to begin
and I am waiting
for the storms of life
to be over
and I am waiting
to set sail for happiness
and I am waiting
for a reconstructed Mayflower
to reach America
with its picture story and tv rights
sold in advance to the natives
and I am waiting
for the lost music to sound again
in the Lost Continent
in a new rebirth of wonder

I am waiting for the day
that maketh all things clear
and I am waiting
for Ole Man River
to just stop rolling along
past the country club
and I am waiting
for the deepest South
to just stop Reconstructing itself
in its own image
and I am waiting
for a sweet desegregated chariot
to swing low
and carry me back to Ole Virginie
and I am waiting
for Ole Virginie to discover
just why Darkies are born
and I am waiting
for God to lookout
from Lookout Mountain
and see the *Ode to the Confederate Dead*
as a real farce
and I am awaiting retribution

for what America did
to Tom Sawyer
and I am perpetually awaiting
a rebirth of wonder

I am waiting for Tom Swift to grow up
and I am waiting
for the American Boy
to take off Beauty's clothes
and get on top of her
and I am waiting
for Alice in Wonderland
to retransmit to me
her total dream of innocence
and I am waiting
for Childe Roland to come
to the final darkest tower
and I am waiting
for Aphrodite
to grow live arms
at a final disarmament conference
in a new rebirth of wonder

I am waiting
to get some intimations
of immortality
by recollecting my early childhood
and I am waiting
for the green mornings to come again
youth's dumb green fields
    come back again
and I am waiting
for some strains of unpremeditated art
to shake my typewriter
and I am waiting to write
the great indelible poem
and I am waiting
for the last long careless rapture
and I am perpetually waiting
for the fleeing lovers
    on the Grecian Urn
to catch each other up at last
and embrace
and I am awaiting
perpetually and forever
a renaissance of wonder

The World's Great Age
Percy Bysshe Shelley
(from *Hellas*)

The world's great age begins anew,
  The golden years return,
The earth doth like a snake renew
  Her winter weeds outworn:
Heaven smiles, and faiths and empires
    gleam,
Like wrecks of a dissolving dream.

A brighter Hellas rears its mountains
  From waves serener far;
A new Peneus rolls his fountains
  Against the morning star.
Where fairer Tempes bloom, there sleep
Young Cyclads on a sunnier deep.

A loftier Argo cleaves the main,
  Fraught with a later prize;
Another Orpheus sings again,
  And loves, and weeps, and dies.
A new Ulysses leaves once more
Calypso for his native shore.

Oh, write no more the tale of Troy,
  If earth Death's scroll must be!
Nor mix with Laian rage the joy
  Which dawns upon the free:
Although a subtler Sphinx renew
Riddles of death Thebes never knew.

Another Athens shall arise,
  And to remoter time
Bequeath, like sunset to the skies,
  The splendour of its prime;
And leave, if naught so bright may live,
All earth can take or Heaven can give.

Saturn and Love their long repose
  Shall burst, more bright and good
Than all who fell, than One who rose,
  Than many unsubdued:
Not gold, not blood, their altar dowers,
But votive tears and symbol flowers.

Oh, cease! must hate and death return?
  Cease! must men kill and die?
Cease! drain not to its dregs the urn
  Of bitter prophecy.
The world is weary of the past,
Oh, might it die or rest at last!

Perspective of the Child

Wonder

Thomas Traherne

How like an angel came I down!
How bright are all things here!
When first among his works I did appear,
Oh, how their glory did me crown;
The world resembled his eternity,
In which my soul did walk;
And ev'rything that I did see
Did with me talk.

The skies in their magnificence,
The lovely lively air,
Oh, how divine, how soft, how sweet, how fair!
The stars did entertain my sense,
And all the works of God so bright and pure,
So rich and great, did seem,
As if they ever must endure
In my esteem.

A native health and innocence
Within my bones did grow,
And while my God did all his glories show,
I felt a vigour in my sense
That was all spirit; I within did flow
With seas of life like wine;
I nothing in the world did know,
But 'twas divine.

Harsh rugged objects were concealed;
Oppressions, tears, and cries,
Sins, griefs, complaints, dissensions, weeping eyes,
Were hid, and only things revealed
Which heavenly spirits and the angels prize:
The state of innocence
And bliss, not trades and poverties,
Did fill my sense.

The streets seemed paved with golden stones,
    The boys and girls all mine—
To me how did their lovely faces shine!
    The sons of men all holy ones,
In joy and beauty then appeared to me;
    And ev'rything I found,
    While like an angel I did see,
        Adorned the ground.

Rich diamonds, and pearl, and gold
    Might ev'rywhere be seen;
Rare colours, yellow, blue, red, white, and green,
    Mine eyes on ev'ry side behold;
All that I saw a wonder did appear,
    Amazement was my bliss,
    That and my wealth met ev'rywhere;
        No joy to this!

Cursed, ill-devised properties,
    With envy, avarice,
And fraud, those fiends that spoil ev'n paradise,
    Were not the object of mine eyes;
Nor hedges, ditches, limits, narrow bounds,
    I dreamt not aught of those,
    But in surveying all men's grounds
        I found repose.

The Game

St. Denys Garneau
(translated by F. R. Scott)

Don't bother me I'm terribly busy

A child is starting to build a village
It's a city, a county
And who knows
Soon the universe.

He's playing

These wooden blocks are houses he moves about and castles
This board is the sign of a sloping roof
not at all bad to look at
It's no small thing to know the place where the road of cards
will turn
This could change completely
the course of the river
Because of the bridge which makes so beautiful a reflection
on the water of the carpet
It's easy to have a tall tree
And to put a mountain underneath
so it'll be high up

Joy of playing! Paradise of liberties!
But above all don't put your foot in the room
One never knows what might be in this corner
Or whether you are not going to crush the favourite
among the invisible flowers

This is my box of toys
Full of words for weaving marvellous patterns
For uniting separating matching
Now the unfolding of the dance
And soon a clear burst of the laughter
That one thought had been lost

A gentle flip of the finger
And the star
Which hung carelessly
At the end of too flimsy a thread of light
Falls and makes rings in the water

Of love and tenderness who would dare to doubt
But not two cents of respect for the established order
Or for politeness and this precious discipline
A levity and practices fit to scandalise grown up people

He arranges words for you as if they were simple songs
And in his eyes one can read his mischievous pleasure
At knowing that under the words he moves everything about
And plays with the mountains
As if they were his very own.
He turns the room upside down and truly we've lost our way
As if it was fun just to fool people.

And yet in his left eye when the right is smiling
A supernatural importance is imparted to the leaf of a tree
As if this could be of great significance
Had as much weight in his scales
As the war of Ethiopia
In England's.

We are not book-keepers

Everyone can see a green dollar bill
But who can see through it
                        except a child
Who like him can see through it with full freedom
Without being in the least hampered by it
                        or its limitations
Or by its value of exactly one dollar

For he sees through this window thousands of marvellous toys
And has no wish to choose between these treasures
Nor desire nor necessity
Not he
For his eyes are wide open to take everything.

Attitude Toward the Body

A Woman Waits for Me
Walt Whitman

A woman waits for me, she contains all, nothing is lacking,
Yet all were lacking if sex were lacking, or if the moisture of
    the right man were lacking.

Sex contains all, bodies, souls,
Meanings, proofs, purities, delicacies, results, promulgations,
Songs, commands, health, pride, the maternal mystery, the
    seminal milk,
All hopes, benefactions, bestowals, all the passions, loves, beauties,
    delights of the earth,
All the governments, judges, gods, follow'd persons of the earth,
These are contain'd in sex as parts of itself and justifications of
    itself.

Without shame the man I like knows and avows the deliciousness
    of his sex,
Without shame the woman I like knows and avows hers.

Now I will dismiss myself from impassive women,
I will go stay with her who waits for me, and with those women
    that are warm-blooded and sufficient for me,
I see that they understand me and do not deny me,
I see that they are worthy of me, I will be the robust husband
    of those women.

They are not one jot less than I am,
They are tann'd in the face by shining suns and blowing winds,
Their flesh has the old divine suppleness and strength,
They know how to swim, row, ride, wrestle, shoot, run, strike,
    retreat, advance, resist, defend themselves,
They are ultimate in their own right—they are calm, clear,
    well-possess'd of themselves.
I draw you close to me, you women,
I cannot let you go, I would do you good,
I am for you, and you are for me, not only for our own sake, but for
    others' sakes,
Envelop'd in you sleep greater heroes and bards,
They refuse to awake at the touch of any man but me.

It is I, you women, I make my way,
I am stern, acrid, large, undissuadable, but I love you,
I do not hurt you any more than is necessary for you,
I pour the stuff to start sons and daughters fit for these States,
    I press with slow rude muscle,
I brace myself effectually, I listen to no entreaties,
I dare not withdraw till I deposit what has so long accumulated
    within me.

Through you I drain the pent-up rivers of myself,
In you I wrap a thousand onward years,
On you I graft the grafts of the best-beloved of me and America,
The drops I distil upon you shall grow fierce and athletic girls, new
    artists, musicians, and singers,
The babes I beget upon you are to beget babes in their turn,
I shall demand perfect men and women out of my love-spendings,
I shall expect them to interpenetrate with others, as I and you
    interpenetrate now,
I shall count on the fruits of the gushing showers of them, as
    I count on the fruits of the gushing showers I give now,
I shall look for loving crops from the birth, life, death, immortality,
    I plant so lovingly now.

The Expense of Spirit in a Waste of Shame
William Shakespeare

The expense of spirit in a waste of shame
Is lust in action, and till action, lust
Is perjured, murderous, bloody, full of blame,
Savage, extreme, rude, cruel, not to trust,
Enjoyed no sooner but despisèd straight,
Past reason hunted, and no sooner had,
Past reason hated, as a swallowed bait,
On purpose laid to make the taker mad.
Mad in pursuit, and in possession so,
Had, having, and in quest to have, extreme,
A bliss in proof, and proved, a very woe.
Before, a joy proposed, behind, a dream.
    All this the world well knows, yet none knows well
    To shun the Heaven that leads men to this Hell.

The Ecstasy
John Donne

Where, like a pillow on a bed,
    A pregnant bank swell'd up to rest
The violet's reclining head,
    Sat we two, one another's best.

Our hands were firmly cemented
    With a fast balm which thence did spring,
Our eye-beams twisted, and did thread
    Our eyes upon one double string;

So t' intergraft our hands, as yet
    Was all the means to make us one,
And pictures on our eyes to get
    Was all our propagation.

As 'twixt two equal armies, fate
    Suspends uncertain victory,
Our souls, which to advance their state
    Were gone out, hung 'twixt her and me.

And whilst our souls negotiate there,
    We like sepulchral statues lay;
All day the same our postures were,
    And we said nothing all the day.

If any (so by love refin'd
    That he soul's language understood,
And by good love were grown all mind)
    Within convenient distance stood,

He (though he knew not which soul spake,
    Because both meant, both spake the same)
Might thence a new concoction take,
    And part far purer than he came.

This ecstasy doth unperplex,
    We said, and tell us what we love;
We see by this it was not sex,
    We see we saw not what did move;

But as all several souls contain
    Mixture of things, they know not what,
Love these mix'd souls doth mix again,
    And makes both one, each this and that.

A single violet transplant,
   The strength, the colour, and the size
(All which before was poor and scant)
   Redoubles still and multiplies.

When love with one another so
   Interinanimates two souls,
That abler soul which thence doth flow
   Defects of loneliness controls.

We then, who are this new soul, know
   Of what we are compos'd and made,
For th' atomies of which we grow
   Are souls, whom no change can invade.

But O, alas, so long, so far
   Our bodies why do we forbear?
They're ours, though they're not we; we are
   Th' intelligences, they the spheres;

We owe them thanks because they thus
   Did us to us at first convey,
Yielded their forces, sense, to us,
   Nor are dross to us, but allay.

On man heaven's influence works not so,
   But that it first imprints the air;
So soul into the soul may flow
   Though it to body first repair.

As our blood labours to beget
   Spirits as like souls as it can,
Because such fingers need to knit
   That subtile knot which makes us man,

So must pure lovers' souls descend
   T' affections and to faculties
Which sense may reach and apprehend;
   Else a great prince in prison lies.

T' our bodies turn we then, that so
   Weak men on love reveal'd may look;
Love's mysteries in souls do grow,
   But yet the body is his book.

And if some lover, such as we,
   Have heard this dialogue of one,
Let him still mark us; he shall see
   Small change when we're to bodies gone.

Attitude Toward Country

Dulce et Decorum Est
Wilfred Owen

Bent double, like old beggars under sacks,
Knock-kneed, coughing like hags, we cursed through sludge,
Till on the haunting flares we turned our backs,
And towards our distant rest began to trudge.
Men marched asleep. Many had lost their boots,
But limped on, blood-shod. All went lame, all blind;
Of gas-shells dropping softly behind.

Gas! Gas! Quick, boys!—An ecstasy of fumbling,
Fitting the clumsy helmets just in time,
But someone still was yelling out and stumbling
And floundering like a man in fire or lime.—
Dim through the misty panes and thick green light,
As under a green sea, I saw him drowning.
In all my dreams before my helpless sight
He plunges at me, guttering, choking, drowning.

If in some smothering dreams, you too could pace
Behind the wagon that we flung him in,
And watch the white eyes writhing in his face,
His hanging face, like a devil's sick of sin;
If you could hear, at every jolt, the blood
Come gargling from the froth-corrupted lungs,
Bitter as the cud
Of vile, incurable sores on innocent tongues,
My friend, you would not tell with such high zest
To children ardent for some desperate glory
The old Lie: Dulce et decorum est
Pro patria mori.

This Royal Throne of Kings

William Shakespeare
(King Richard II, Act II, sc. 1, 11.40-68)

This royal throne of kings, this scepter'd isle,
This earth of majesty, this seat of Mars,
This other Eden, demi-paradise;
This fortress built by Nature for herself
Against infection and the hand of war;
This happy breed of men, this little world;
This precious stone set in the silver sea,
Which serves it in the office of a wall,
Or as a moat defensive to a house,
Against the envy of less happier lands;
This blessed plot, this earth, this realm, this England,
This nurse, this teeming womb of royal kings,
Fear'd by their breed and famous by their birth,
Renowned for their deeds as far from home,
For Christian service and true chivalry,
As is the sepulchre in stubborn Jewry
Of the world's ransom, blessed Mary's Son;
This land of such dear souls, this dear dear land,
Dear for her reputation through the world,
Is now leased out—I die pronouncing it—
Like to a tenement or pelting farm:
England, bound in with the triumphant sea,
Whose rocky shore beats back the envious siege
Of watery Neptune, is now bound in with shame,
With inky blots and rotten parchment bonds:
That England, that was wont to conquer others,
Hath made a shameful conquest of itself.
Ah, would the scandal vanish with my life,
How happy then were my ensuing death?

Perspective of the Puritan

One Home
William Stafford

Mine was a Midwest home—you can keep your world.
Plain black hats rode the thoughts that made our code.
We sang hymns in the house; the roof was near God.

The light bulb that hung in the pantry made a wan light,
but we could read by it the names of preserves—
outside, the buffalo grass, and the wind in the night.

A wildcat sprang at Grandpa on the Fourth of July
when he was cutting plum bushes for fuel,
before Indians pulled the West over the edge of the sky.

To anyone who looked at us we said, 'My friend';
liking the cut of a thought, we could say 'Hello'.
(But plain black hats rode the thoughts that made our code.)

The sun was over our town; it was like a blade.
Kicking cottonwood leaves we ran toward storms.
Wherever we looked the land would hold us up.

The Lotos-Eaters
Alfred, Lord Tennyson
(Lines 153-173)

Let us swear an oath, and keep it with an equal mind,
In the hollow Lotos-land to live and lie reclined
On the hills like gods together, careless of mankind.
For they lie beside their nectar, and the bolts are hurled
Far below them in the valleys, and the clouds are lightly curled
Round their golden houses, girdled with the gleaming world:
Where they smile in secret, looking over wasted lands,
Blight and famine, plague and earthquake, roaring deeps and fiery sands,
Clanging fights, and flaming towns, and sinking ships, and praying hands.
But they smile, they find a music centred in a doleful song
Steaming up, a lamentation and an ancient tale of wrong,
Like a tale of little meaning though the words are strong;
Chanted from an ill-used race of men that cleave the soil,
Sow the seed, and reap the harvest with enduring toil,
Storing yearly little dues of wheat, and wine and oil;
Till they perish and they suffer—some, 'tis whispered—down in hell
Suffer endless anguish, others in Elysian valleys dwell,
Resting weary limbs at last on beds of asphodel.
Surely, surely, slumber is more sweet than toil, the shore
Than labour in the deep mid-ocean, wind and wave and oar;
O rest ye, brother mariners, we will not wander more.

The Hazard of Loving the Creatures
Isaac Watts

Where e'er my flatt'ring Passions rove
   I find a lurking Snare;
'Tis dangerous to let loose our Love
   Beneath th' Eternal Fair.

Souls whom the Tye of Friendship binds,
   And Partners of our Blood,
Seize a large Portion of our Minds,
   And leave the less for God.

Nature has soft but powerful Bands,
   And Reason she controuls;
While Children with their little Hands
   Hang closest to our Souls.

Thoughtless they act th' old Serpents Part;
   What tempting things they be!
Lord, how they twine about our Heart,
   And draw it off from thee!

Our hasty Wills rush blindly on
   Where rising Passion rolls,
And thus we make our Fetters strong
   To bind our slavish Souls.

Dear Sovereign, break these Fetters off,
   And set our Spirits free;
God in himself is Bliss enough,
   For we have all in thee.

Morning-Glory

Words and Music by Tim Buckley
Goodbye and Hello, Electra EKS 7318

I lit my purest candle close to my
Window, hoping it would catch the eye
Of any vagabond who passed it by,
And I waited in my fleeting house

Before he came I felt him drawing near;
As he neared I felt the ancient fear
That he had come to wound my door and jeer,
And I waited in my fleeting house

"Tell me stories," I called to the Hobo;
"Stories of cold," I smiled at the Hobo;
"Stories of old," I knelt to the Hobo;
And he stood before my fleeting house

"No," said the Hobo, "No more tales of time;
Don't ask me now to wash away the grime;
I can't come in 'cause it's too high a climb,"
And he walked away from my fleeting house

"Then you be damned!" I screamed to the Hobo;
"Leave me alone," I wept to the Hobo;
"Turn into stone," I knelt to the Hobo;
And he walked away from my fleeting house

Effort at Speech Between Two People
Muriel Rukeyser

Speak to me.   Take my hand.   What are you now?
I will tell you all.   I will conceal nothing.
When I was three, a little child read a story about a rabbit
who died, in the story, and I crawled under a chair:
a pink rabbit: it was my birthday, and a candle
burnt a sore spot on my finger, and I was told to be happy.

Oh, grow to know me.   I am not happy.   I will be open:
Now I am thinking of white sails against a sky like music,
like glad horns blowing, and birds tilting, and an arm about me.
There was one I loved, who wanted to live, sailing.

Speak to me.   Take my hand.   What are you now?
When I was nine, I was fruitily sentimental,
fluid: and my widowed aunt played Chopin,
and I bent my head on the painted woodwork, and wept.
I want now to be close to you.   I would
link the minutes of my days close, somehow, to your days.

I am not happy.   I will be open.
I have liked lamps in evening corners, and quiet poems.
There has been fear in my life.   Sometimes I speculate
On what a tragedy his life was, really.

Take my hand.   Fist my mind in your hand.   What are you now?
When I was fourteen, I had dreams of suicide,
and I stood at a steep window, at sunset, hoping toward death:
if the light had not melted clouds and plains to beauty,
if light had not transformed that day, I would have leapt,
I am unhappy.   I am lonely.   Speak to me.

I will be open.   I think he never loved me:
he loved the bright beaches, the little lips of foam
that ride small waves, he loved the veer of gulls:
he said with a gay mouth: I love you.   Grow to know me.

What are you now?   If we could touch one another,
if these our separate entities could come to grips,
clenched like a Chinese puzzle . . . yesterday
I stood in a crowded street that was live with people,
and no one spoke a word, and the morning shone.
Everyone silent, moving. . . . Take my hand.   Speak to me.

The Coming of the Magi
Raymond Souster

In the tableau *The Coming of the Magi*
The Wise Men are seen at the entrance to the manger
Holding out precious gifts, gold,
Frankincense and myrrh, a look
Of awe and joy on their faces. . . .
                    "Trouble with them guys",
He tells her, watching her last
Tantalizing twist from the girdle—
"They never had anything like this
To keep them home nights."
                    "Like what?" she teases,
But he's looking out the window across to the church
Where the floodlights show up the awkward scene at the manger.

"Like what?" she repeats, taking care rolling down the second stocking.

"Like what, like what," he mocks her:
"Hell, think of them guys giving all that stuff
To a kid like Jesus. . . ."

No Man Can Find the War
Words and Music by Tim Buckley
Goodbye and Hello, Electra EKS 7318

Photographs of guns and flame
Scarlet skull and distant game
Bayonet and jungle grin
Nightmares dreamed by bleeding men
Lookouts tremble on the shore
But no man can find the war

Tape recorders echo scream
Orders fly like bullet stream
Drums and cannons laugh aloud
Whistles come from ashen shroud
Leaders damn the world and roar
But no man can find the war

Is the war across the sea?
Is the war behind the sky?
Have you each and all gone blind:
Is the war inside your mind?

Humans weep at human death
All the talkers lose their breath
Movies paint a chaos tale
Singers see and poets wail
All the world knows the score
But no man can find the war

War
Langston Hughes

The face of war is my face.
The face of war is your face.
    What color
    Is the face
    Of war?
Brown, black, white—
Your face and my face.

Death is the broom
I take in my hands
To sweep the world
    Clean.
I sweep and I sweep
Then mop and I mop.
I dip my broom in blood,
My mop in blood—
And blame you for this,
Because you are *there,*
    Enemy.

It's hard to blame me,
Because I am here—
So I kill you.
And you kill me.
    My name,
Like your name,
    Is war.

Once I Was

Words and Music by Tim Buckley
Goodbye and Hello, Elektra EKS 7318

*Once I was a soldier
And I fought on foreign sands for you
Once I was a hunter
And I brought home fresh meat for you
Once I was a lover
And I searched behind
    your eyes for you
And soon there'll be another
To tell you I was just a lie*

*And sometimes I wonder
Just for awhile
Will you ever remember me*

*And though you have forgotten
All of our rubbish dreams
I find myself searching
Through the ashes of our ruins
For the days when we smiled
And the hours that ran wild
With the magic of our eyes
And the silence of our words*

*And sometimes I wonder
Just for awhile
Will you ever remember me*

The Definition of Love

Andrew Marvell

My love is of a birth as rare
As 'tis for object strange and high;
It was begotten by despair
Upon impossibility.

Magnanimous despair alone
Could show me so divine a thing,
Where feeble hope could ne'er have flown,
But vainly flapped its tinsel wing.

And yet I quickly might arrive
Where my extended soul is fixed
But fate does iron wedges drive,
And always crowds itself betwixt.

For fate with jealous eye does see
Two perfect loves, nor lets them close;
Their union would her ruin be,
And her tyrannic power depose.

And therefore her decrees of steel
Us as the distant poles have placed,
Though love's whole world on us doth wheel,
Not by themselves to be embraced;

Unless the giddy heaven fall,
And earth some new convulsion tear,
And, us to join, the world should all
Be cramped into a planisphere.

As lines, so loves, oblique may well
Themselves in every angle greet;
But ours so truly parallel,
Though infinite, can never meet.

Therefore the love which doth us bind,
But fate so enviously debars,
Is the conjunction of the mind,
And opposition of the stars.

4

Joni Mitchell

Unlike most of her contemporaries, Joni Mitchell manages to write verse of enchanting subtlety without deflecting our attention away from melody, mainly because her melody is as subtle as her verse, every melodic motion and gesture perfectly matched with the turns of her words. What is the secret of this lyrical magic? Perhaps what first strikes us when we hear a Joni Mitchell song is her imagery. New York is a place where "the stars paid a light bill" *(Song to a Seagull)*; summer "falls to the sidewalk like string and brown paper" *(Marcie);* and "an aging cripple" can be seen "selling Superman ballons" *(Nathan La Franeer).* Here are objects we can see with our eyes, minds, and feelings. Because of the opposition between the elements united in them, they also surprise us into asking questions. But the wonder-work done by these images is not due solely to their internal content and structure. By far the greatest part of that work results from the release her images provide for the poetic energy she generates in the *contexts* of the images.

For the sake of those who wish to write poetry and those who want simply to sharpen their awareness of it, we shall present here a detailed analysis of the contexts controlling the development of Joni Mitchell's songs. We shall consider how she achieves her effects by discussing five general contexts of poetry: attitude, manner, style, thought, description and narration, and representation.

Attitude
For Joni Mitchell's songs, the most important context is the *attitude* she takes toward her material. Her attitude is primarily lyrical, her work being experienced principally as an expression of a personal feeling or state of mind. Not just any attitude will do in writing lyrical poetry. If we sense that the poet is merely gushing or raging, for example, we will pull back. An attitude that has internal tension is most effective. Such tension is immediately interesting and provides a natural basis for developing the conflict that all poems require if they are to live. Joni

Mitchell's attitude is of this sort. In one way intimately involved in all she says and sings, and yet, on another level always carefully distanced from her material, she projects an ambivalence that is exquisitely intriguing. Of course we are not speaking here of Joni Mitchell the person. All that is aesthetically relevant is Joni Mitchell as she reveals herself in her songs. In the attitude of this "apparent" personality a polarization takes place between involvement and detachment, naivete and awareness, sensitivity and tough-mindedness, child and woman. There is, however, no confusion in these oppositions. Throughout each song we sense their fusion in the sustained mood of gentle irony playing under her imagery.

Manner

The way that the tension within Joni Mitchell's attitude shapes the other contexts of her work can be seen first in the general *manner* in which she expresses her feelings and state of mind. Compelling her to talk with someone, her inner tension is such that the person spoken to should be neither (at least not directly) a lover (for that would be too intimate) nor the general public (for that would be too distant). The right balance is hit when she takes her audience to be her friend and makes her form of communication something like a personal letter, which she either addresses directly to the friend, as in *Nathan La Franeer, Michael from Mountains,* and *Marcie,* or which she shows to the friend after writing it to someone else, as in *Song to a Seagull.* Of course, her poems are not really personal letters to or for a friend. They are essentially descriptive and narrative songs. But they have the effect of personal letters, for they speak of places she's been, people she's known, things she's seen—bits of ordinary life she herself has lived and is now telling about in the sort of colloquial language a good friend expects to hear. The song-letter form, however, is not merely appropriate for the attitude she takes toward her material. It carries its own interest, for it both heightens the credibility of the content and teases us with the distance it places between us and the delightful character who is trying to communicate with us.

Style

We might next consider how Joni's attitude shapes the *style* of the song-letters. Pressure from the open, child-like side of her nature is felt in her light, conversational idioms, in phrases like "silly seabird," "night in the city looks pretty to me," and "yellow slickers up on swings." Against this language of spontaneous response work the sharp intellectual observations she makes from her other side—the Joni Mitchell who appears to keep life removed from herself so that she can know it in freedom. The result is a continual tension between intimate, colloquial expression and a contrapuntal irony. To appreciate the interest that this tension in her style creates, one need only consider what would happen to her songs if she simply proclaimed her views, or milked her audience for sympathy instead of engaging them to share with her the bitter-sweet humor of things.

Thought
The irony characterizing Joni's style operates not only in individual observations she makes about her subject matter, but also through the general view of life that motivates her to make them. Technically, this aspect is usually called the context of *thought.* Ironic thought in Joni Mitchell's song-poems is not, however, unmitigated. Again in keeping with the duality of her attitude, while she sees, without withdrawing into pessimism, the ironic disparity between human aspirations and what is in fact attainable, her joy in life is too great to be defeated by her sceptical intellect. There is no suggestion, for example, that it would have been wiser for the deserted Marcie not to have hoped for her lover's return, or for Joni not to have identified with the seagull; nor even in the bitter *Nathan La Franeer* does the ugliness of New York completely excuse the cab driver for his unkindness.

Description and Narration
We come next to the question of how the thought behind Joni Mitchell's poems is artistically realized. The simplest way of implementing thought is through straight argument. But argument would not express what Joni has to say. Standing aside, she lets her material speak for itself through word-sketches of persons, places, and things, and "word-films" of events. The word-films are the most important. Through them a brief moment in time can suggest a much larger pattern of activity, which in turn becomes the object of the thought in the poem. In *Nathan La Franeer,* Joni is on her way to the airport; in *Song to a Seagull,* she visits the seashore; and in *Michael from Mountains,* a little boy is going home in the rain.

In each of these vignettes of daily routine, a whole way of life and a whole set of relations to existence are revealed. Consider, for example, these lines in *Michael from Mountains:*

There's oil on the puddles in taffeta patterns
That run down the drain
In colored arrangements
That Michael will change with a stick that he found.

What sort of a person would pay such attention to oily puddles and a boy fiddling with a stick? Only someone with a quiet passion for "useless" surfaces. Michael, too, is obviously a lover of colors and patterns, but his love is the active wonder of the child. The difference between them, however, only underscores what they share: a playful reverence for being.

Representation
Joni's suggestively anecdotal *representation* evidences again the intriguing manner in which she is continually feeling her way between remoteness and involvement. As is usual in songwriting, her music consists of tightly balanced repetitions and variations of a common theme, and consequently the lyrics welded to the music must also be developed in that fashion. But there are few songwriters whose lyrics take such subtle advantage of that confinement. In her hands, the verses that must be balanced for the sake of the music often become delicately juxtaposed scenes that in contrast to one another expose the detailed working of change on people we might watch from windows. In other words, Joni makes the balance and distance inherent in the song form perfect expressions of her reflective approach to her material, while at the same time her love of life finds its way out through the care with which she observes.

The beginning and final verses of *Marcie* provide a good illustration of this representational technique. We first see Marcie trying to make time pass while she waits for word from her lover; in the last verse, however, we don't see her at all—we just learn that "someone heard she bought a one-way ticket/and went west again." Joni stops short of showing us Marcie's final despair, out of respect, perhaps, both for her protagonist and her audience's imagination.

In any event, the distancing of the little tragedy produces an effect typical of Joni's songwriting, a poignancy that outlasts sorrow.

The second aspect of her technique, the care she feels toward her material, is shown in the tender realism of the poetic details. Marcie does not begin in simple hope; that would be false to life and to art, for the beginning would then not contain the grounds for the ending. Hope is there only implicitly, in the "coat of flowers" she wears, and the man's shirt she uses to "dust her tables". What dominates is the impression of empty daily routine into which Marcie, not without bravery, is trying to escape, an impression which provides the theme that the rest of the song develops musically and lyrically.

When we move from the verse-scenes of Joni's songs to her individual lines, we can find everywhere examples of this combination of reflective juxtapositioning and warm, concerned observation. Watch, for instance, what happens to the words "red" and "green" in *Marcie*. But perhaps enough has been said to support our main thesis, namely, that the sources of the power in Joni's imagery are not only in the images themselves, but also in the contexts that control the images. In her song-poems, the contexts of attitude, manner, thought, narration, and representation each have their own interest; and because of the organic way in which they connect with one another, these contexts also concentrate their interests into unified appeals which it is the task of the images to communicate.

In the following section the student can gain further insight into the possibilities of treating imagery by considering the poems associated with *Song to a Seagull*. Joni Mitchell's song and the related poems illustrate what can be done with one basic image, the bird-figure of countless myths and daydreams.

Marcie

Words and Music by Joni Mitchell
Joni Mitchell, Reprise S 6293

Marcie in a coat of flowers
Stops inside a candy store
Reds are sweet and greens are sour
Still no letter at her door
So she'll wash her flower curtains
Hang them in the wind to dry
Dust her tables with his shirt and
Wave another day goodbye

Marcie's faucet needs a plumber
Marcie's sorrow needs a man
Red is autumn green is summer
Greens are turning and the sand
All along the ocean beaches
Stares up empty at the sky
Marcie buys a bag of peaches
Stops a postman passing by
And summer goes
Falls to the sidewalk like string and brown paper
Winter blows
Up from the river there's no one to take her
To the sea

Marcie dresses warm it's snowing
Takes a yellow cab uptown
Red is stop and green's for going
Sees a show and rides back down
Down along the Hudson River
Past the shipyards in the cold
Still no letter's been delivered
Still the winter days unfold
Like magazines
Fading in dusty grey attics and cellars
Make a dream
Dream back to summer and hear how he tells her
Wait for me

Marcie leaves and doesn't tell us
Where or why she moved away
Red is angry green is jealous
That was all she had to say
Someone thought they saw her Sunday
Window shopping in the rain
Someone heard she bought a one-way ticket
And went west again

Patterns

Amy Lowell

I walk down the garden paths,
And all the daffodils
Are blowing, and the bright blue squills.
I walk down the patterned garden-paths
In my stiff, brocaded gown.
With my powdered hair and jewelled fan,
I too am a rare
Pattern. As I wander down
The garden paths.

My dress is richly figured,
And the train
Makes a pink and silver stain
On the gravel, and the thrift
Of the borders.
Just a plate of current fashion,
Tripping by in high-heeled, ribboned shoes.
Not a softness anywhere about me,
Only whalebone and brocade.
And I sink on a seat in the shade
Of a lime tree. For my passion
Wars against the stiff brocade.
The daffodils and squills
Flutter in the breeze
As they please.
And I weep;
For the lime-tree is in blossom
And one small flower has dropped upon my bosom.

And the plashing of waterdrops
In the marble fountain
Comes down the garden-paths.
The dripping never stops.
Underneath my stiffened gown
Is the softness of a woman bathing in a marble basin,
A basin in the midst of hedges grown
So thick, she cannot see her lover hiding,
But she guesses he is near,
And the sliding of the water
Seems the stroking of a dear
Hand upon her.
What is Summer in a fine brocaded gown!
I should like to see it lying in a heap upon the ground.
All the pink and silver crumpled up on the ground.

I would be the pink and silver as I ran along the paths,
And he would stumble after,
Bewildered by my laughter.
I should see the sun flashing from his sword-hilt and the
        buckles on his shoes.
I would choose
To lead him in a maze along the patterned paths,
A bright and laughing maze for my heavy-booted lover.
Till he caught me in the shade,
And the buttons of his waistcoat bruised my body as he
        clasped me,
Aching, melting, unafraid.
With the shadows of the leaves and the sundrops,
And the plopping of the waterdrops,
All about us in the open afternoon—
I am very like to swoon
With the weight of this brocade,
For the sun sifts through the shade.

Underneath the fallen blossom
In my bosom,
Is a letter I have hid.
It was brought to me this morning by a rider from the Duke.
'Madam, we regret to inform you that Lord Hartwell
Died in action Thursday se'nnight.'
As I read it in the white, morning sunlight,
The letters squirmed like snakes.
'Any answer, Madam,' said my footman.
'No,' I told him.
'See that the messenger takes some refreshment.

No, no answer.'
And I walked into the garden,
Up and down the patterned paths,
In my stiff, correct brocade.
The blue and yellow flowers stood up proudly in the sun.
Each one.
I stood upright too,
Held rigid to the pattern
By the stiffness of my gown.
Up and down I walked,
Up and down.

In a month he would have been my husband.
In a month, here, underneath this lime,
We would have broke the pattern;
He for me, and I for him,
He as Colonel, I as Lady,
On this shady seat.
He had a whim
That sunlight carried blessing.
And I answered, 'It shall be as you have said.'
Now he is dead.

In Summer and in Winter I shall walk
Up and down
The patterned garden-paths
In my stiff, brocaded gown.
The squills and daffodils
Will give place to pillared roses, and to asters, and to snow.
I shall go
Up and down,
In my gown.
Gorgeously arrayed,
Boned and stayed.
And the softness of my body will be guarded from embrace
By each button, hook, and lace.
For the man who should loose me is dead,
Fighting with the Duke in Flanders,
In a pattern called a war.
Christ! What are patterns for?

Michael from Mountains

Words and Music by Joni Mitchell
Joni Mitchell, Reprise S 6293

Michael wakes you up with sweets
He takes you up street and the rain comes down
Sidewalk markets locked up tight
And umbrellas bright on a grey background
There's oil on the puddles in taffeta patterns
That run down the drain
In colored arrangements
That Michael will change with a stick that he found.

Chorus:

Michael from mountains
Go where you will go to
Know that I will know you
Someday I may know you very well

Michael brings you to a park
He sings and it's dark when the clouds come by
Yellow slickers up on swings
Like puppets on strings hanging in the sky
They'll splash home to suppers in wallpapered kitchens
Their mothers will scold
But Michael will hold you
To keep away cold till the sidewalks are dry

Chorus

Michael leads you up the stairs
He needs you to care and you know you do
Cats come crying to the key
And dry you will be in a towel or two
There's rain in the window
There's sun in the painting that smiles on the wall
You want to know all
But his mountains have called so you never do

Chorus

Ode: Intimations of Immortality

William Wordsworth
(stanzas VII and VIII)

Behold the Child among his new-born blisses,
A six years' darling of a pigmy size!
See, where 'mid work of his own hand he lies,
Fretted by sallies of his mother's kisses,
With light upon him from his father's eyes!
See, at his feet, some little plan or chart,
Some fragment from his dream of human life,
Shaped by himself with newly-learnèd art;
    A wedding or a festival,
    A mourning or a funeral;
      And this hath now his heart,
    And unto this he frames his song:
      Then will he fit his tongue
To dialogues of business, love, or strife;
    But it will not be long
    Ere this be thrown aside,
    And with new joy and pride
The little Actor cons another part;
Filling from time to time his 'humorous stage'
With all the Persons, down to palsied Age,
That Life brings with her in her equipage;
    As if his whole vocation
    Were endless imitation.

Thou, whose exterior semblance doth belie
    Thy soul's immensity;
Thou best philosopher, who yet dost keep
Thy heritage, thou eye among the blind,
That, deaf and silent, read'st the Eternal Deep,
Haunted forever by the Eternal Mind,—
    Mighty prophet! seer blest!
    On whom those truths do rest,
Which we are toiling all our lives to find,
In darkness lost, the darkness of the grave;
Thou, over whom thy Immortality
Broods like the Day, a master o'er a slave,
A Presence which is not to be put by;
Thou little Child, yet glorious in the might
Of heaven-born freedom on thy being's height,

Why with such earnest pains dost thou provoke
The years to bring the inevitable yoke,
Thus blindly with thy blessedness at strife?
Full soon thy Soul shall have her earthly freight,
And custom lie upon thee with a weight,
Heavy as frost, and deep almost as life!

Nathan La Franeer

Words and Music by Joni Mitchell
Joni Mitchell, Reprise S 6293

I hired a coach to take me from confusion to the plane
And though we shared a common space I know I'll never meet again
The driver with his eyebrows furrowed in the rear-view mirror
I read his name and it was plainly written Nathan La Franeer

I asked him would he hurry
But we crawled the canyons slowly
Through the buyers and the sellers
Through the burglar bells and the wishing wells
With gangs and girly shows
The ghostly garden grows

The cars and buses bustled through the bedlam of the day
I looked through window-glass at streets and Nathan grumbled at the grey
I saw an aging cripple selling Superman balloons
The city grate through chrome-plate
The clock struck slowly half-past-noon
Through the tunnel tiled and turning
Into daylight once again I am escaping
Once again goodbye
To symphonies and dirty trees
With parks and plastic clothes
The ghostly garden grows

He asked me for a dollar more
He cursed me to my face
He hated everyone who paid to ride
And share his common space
I picked my bags up from the curb
And stumbled to the door
Another man reached out his hand
Another hand reached out for more
And I filled it full of silver
And I left the fingers counting
And the sky goes on forever
Without metermaids and peace parades
You feed it all your woes
The ghostly garden grows

London
William Blake

I wander thro' each charter'd street,
Near where the charter'd Thames does flow,
And mark in every face I meet
Marks of weakness, marks of woe.

In every cry of every Man,
In every Infant's cry of fear,
In every voice, in every ban,
The mind-forg'd manacles I hear.

How the Chimney-sweeper's cry
Every black'ning Church appalls;
And the hapless Soldier's sigh
Runs in blood down Palace walls.

But most thro' midnight streets I hear
How the youthful Harlot's curse
Blasts the new born Infant's tear,
And blights with plagues the Marriage hearse.

Sion Lies Waste

Fulke Greville

Sion lies waste, and thy Jerusalem,
O Lord, is fallen to utter desolation;
Against thy prophets and thy holy men
The sin hath wrought a fatal combination;
   Profaned thy name, thy worship overthrown,
   And made thee, living Lord, a God unknown.

Thy powerful laws, thy wonders of creation,
Thy word incarnate, glorious heaven, dark hell,
Lie shadowed under man's degeneration;
Thy Christ still crucified for doing well;
   Impiety, O Lord, sits on thy throne,
   Which makes thee, living light, a God unknown.

Man's superstition hath thy truths entombed,
His atheism again her pomps defaceth;
That sensual unsatiable vast womb
Of thy seen church thy unseen church disgraceth.
   There lives no truth with them that seem thine own,
   Which makes thee, living Lord, a God unknown.

Yet unto thee, Lord, mirror of transgression,
We who for earthly idols have forsaken
Thy heavenly image, sinless, pure impression,
And so in nets of vanity lie taken,
   All desolate implore that to thine own,
   Lord, thou no longer live a God unknown.

Yet, Lord, let Israel's plagues not be eternal,
Nor sin forever cloud thy sacred mountains,
Nor with false flames, spiritual but infernal,
Dry up thy mercy's ever springing fountains.
   Rather, sweet Jesus, fill up time and come
   To yield the sin her everlasting doom.

Song to a Seagull

Words and Music by Joni Mitchell
Joni Mitchell, Reprise S 6293

Fly silly seabird
No dreams can possess you
No voices can blame you
For sun on your wings
My gentle relations
Have names they must call me
For loving the freedom
Of all flying things
My dreams with the seagulls fly

Out of reach out of cry
I came to the city
And lived like Old Crusoe
On an island of noise
In a cobblestone sea
And the beaches were concrete
And the stars paid a light bill
And the blossoms hung false
On their store window trees
My dreams with the seagulls fly
Out of reach out of cry

Out of the city
And down to the seaside
To sun on my shoulders
And wind in my hair
But sandcastles crumble
And hunger is human
And humans are hungry
For worlds they can't share
My dreams with the seagulls fly

Out of reach out of cry
I call to the seagull
Who dives to the waters
And catches his silver-fine
Dinner alone
Crying where are the footprints
That danced on these beaches
And the hands that cast wishes
That sunk like a stone
My dreams with the seagulls fly
Out of reach out of cry

Tern

John Bruce

Every year at this time and on this windless sort of evening
The single tern fishes across from me on the same flat bay;
In measure after measure and mismeasured swoops and feints
It shapes and arcs at the sheen and silver beneath his eye;
And on the last furring of light I can see his finned wing
Cut above the trees and away down as old as myth,
As cold white as Greece's last great murmurations of art.

Ode to a Nightingale
John Keats

My heart aches, and a drowsy numbness pains
  My sense, as though of hemlock I had drunk,
Or emptied some dull opiate to the drains
  One minute past, and Lethe-wards had sunk:
'Tis not through envy of thy happy lot,
  But being too happy in thine happiness,—
    That thou, light-winged Dryad of the trees,
      In some melodious plot
  Of beechen green, and shadows numberless,
    Singest of summer in full-throated ease.

O for a draught of vintage! that hath been
  Cooled a long age in the deep-delved earth,
Tasting of Flora and the country green,
  Dance, and Provençal song, and sunburnt mirth!
O for a beaker full of the warm South,
  Full of the true, the blushful Hippocrene,
    With beaded bubbles winking at the brim,
      And purple-stained mouth;
  That I might drink, and leave the world unseen,
    And with thee fade away into the forest dim:

Fade far away, dissolve, and quite forget
  What thou among the leaves hast never known,
The weariness, the fever, and the fret
  Here, where men sit and hear each other groan;
Where palsy shakes a few, sad, last gray hairs,
  Where youth grows pale, and spectre-thin, and dies;
    Where but to think is to be full of sorrow
      And leaden-eyed despairs,
  Where Beauty cannot keep her lustrous eyes,
    Or new Love pine at them beyond tomorrow.

Away! away! for I will fly to thee,
  Not charioted by Bacchus and his pards,
But on the viewless wings of Poesy,
  Though the dull brain perplexes and retards:
Already with thee! tender is the night,
  And haply the Queen-Moon is on her throne,
    Clustered around by all her starry Fays;
      But here there is no light,
Save what from heaven is with the breezes blown
    Through verdurous glooms and winding mossy ways.

I cannot see what flowers are at my feet,
  Nor what soft incense hangs upon the boughs,
But, in embalmed darkness, guess each sweet
  Wherewith the seasonable month endows
The grass, the thicket, and the fruit-tree wild;
  White hawthorn, and the pastoral eglantine;
    Fast-fading violets covered up in leaves;
      And mid-May's eldest child,
  The coming musk-rose, full of dewy wine,
    The murmurous haunt of flies on summer eves.

Darkling I listen; and for many a time
  I have been half in love with easeful Death,
Called him soft names in many a mused rhyme,
  To take into the air my quiet breath;
Now more than ever seems it rich to die,
  To cease upon the midnight with no pain,
    While thou art pouring forth thy soul abroad
      In such an ecstasy!
  Still wouldst thou sing, and I have ears in vain—
    To thy high requiem become a sod.

Thou wast not born for death, immortal Bird!
  No hungry generations tread thee down;
The voice I hear this passing night was heard
  In ancient days by emperor and clown:
Perhaps the self-same song that found a path
  Through the sad heart of Ruth, when, sick for home,
    She stood in tears amid the alien corn,
      The same that oft-times hath
  Charmed magic casements, opening on the foam
    Of perilous seas, in faery lands forlorn.

Forlorn! the very word is like a bell
  To toll me back from thee to my sole self!
Adieu! the fancy cannot cheat so well
  As she is famed to do, deceiving elf.
Adieu! adieu! thy plaintive anthem fades
  Past the near meadows, over the still stream,
    Up the hill-side; and now 'tis buried deep
      In the next valley-glades:
  Was it a vision, or a waking dream?
    Fled is that music:—Do I wake or sleep?

Nun on a Beach
John Harney

Birds, black or white, both;
They wheel:
    one like a dervish
    on the windy beach,
    a nun flailing at
    the lusty afternoon,
    blushing for the waves
    that leer and kiss and toss
    on their heavy sea-grown beds.

The other is a bird;
    gull, white and whistling,
    an improbable yellow
    horn for a beak, eyes
    glowing with love's improper
    hue, bestial ruddy red;
    scavenger, gleaner of refuse,
    his feathers belie his dusty trade.

Today she gleans on the shores of heaven,
And he's in his paradise;
    for both, black or white,
    the almighty is a fish:
    once, to be caught alive,
    twice, to be eaten dead,
    and three, as ever, or always,
    swimming in a mystery.

Night in the City

Words and Music by Joni Mitchell
Joni Mitchell, Reprise S 6293

Light up, light up
Light up you lazy blue eyes
Moon's up, night's up
Taking the town by surprise

Night time, night time
Day left an hour ago
City light time
Must you get ready so slow?
There are places to come from
And places to go

Night in the city looks pretty to me
Night in the city looks fine
Music comes spilling out into the street
Colors go flashing in time

Take off, take off
Take off those stay-at-home blues
Break off, shake off
Take off those stay-at-home blues
Stairway, stairway
Down to the crowds in the street
They go their way
Looking for faces to greet
But we run on laughing with no one to meet

Night in the city looks pretty to me
Night in the city looks fine
Music comes spilling out into the street
Colors go waltzing in time

Composed Upon Westminster Bridge

William Wordsworth

Earth has not anything to show more fair:
Dull would he be of soul who could pass by
A sight so touching in its majesty:
This city now doth like a garment wear
The beauty of the morning; silent, bare,
Ships, towers, domes, theatres,

Open unto the fields, and to the sky;
All bright and glittering in the smokeless air.

Never did sun more beautifully steep
In his first splendour valley, rock, or hill;
Ne'er saw I, never felt, a calm so deep!
The river glideth at his own sweet will:
Dear God! the very houses seem asleep;
And all that mighty heart is lying still!

5

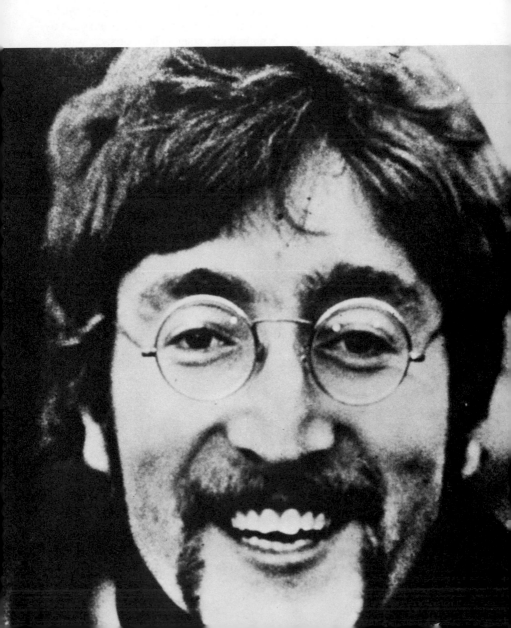

John Lennon
and the Beatles

Of the many controversies surrounding the Beatles, one
that is especially interesting for us concerns the signifi-
cance of a now famous line in John Lennon's and Paul
McCartney's song, *A Day in the Life.* Suddenly interrupting
his autobiography of a totally inauthentic existence, the
protagonist of the song turns to his audience and says,
"I'd love to turn you on." The line is repeated at the end of
the song, and on the word "on," a massive cacophony,
involving a 40-piece orchestra, crescendoes into an
overwhelming wall of sound, after which a single chord
trails off at length into a realm beyond hearing, closing
both the song and the album, *Sgt. Pepper's Lonely Hearts
Club Band.*

Now the question is this: how are we to take that line?
Is it a call to enjoy all that life can be? If so, then the
protagonist is either being remarkably out of character
when he speaks the line, or a new voice is here introduced,
perhaps that of the author himself. Or is this line the
climactic revelation of how modern Everyman is being
destroyed by his inability to relate to anything but kicks?
But if that is the answer, then the astonishing excitement
of the accompanying music must be regarded as a trap for
the listener, a demonstration of how he too can be taken in
by the rages of our time.

And there are other explanations that seem plausible.
The BBC banned *A Day in the Life* because it was
convinced the line, "I'd love to turn you on," referred to
LSD. According to Hunter Davies, the "official" Beatles'
biographer, Paul McCartney says the line refers to
" 'turning people on to the truth about themselves'—to
make them see how materialistic they are." (*Life*,
September 20, 1968). Then again, there is the possibility
that the line is a "con". Davies reports John Lennon as
having this to say about the way the Beatles write for
their audience:

"We know we're conning them, because we know
people want to be conned. Let's stick that in there, we
say. That'll start them puzzling. I bet Picasso sticks
things in. I bet he's been laughing about it for the last
80 years. Beethoven is a con, just like we are now.
He was just knocking out a bit of work, that was all."
(Loc. cit.)

The difficulties raised by the line, "I'd love to turn you on,"
typify the problems faced by any would-be interpreter of
the Beatles. Continually he will be caught between two
sets of facts: a multiplicity of possible interpretations and
the persistent tendency of people to sense significance in
Beatles' lyrics. To account for these facts, he will need to
recognize a special kind of ambiguity running through
*A Day in the Life, Eleanor Rigby, Lucy in the Sky with
Diamonds,* and nearly all the other Lennon and McCartney
songs whose lyrics are especially compelling. This
ambiguity may not be definable, but it can be partially
described.

In the first place, ambiguity, or the possibility of more than
one meaning for a given set of words, does not function
for Lennon's and McCartney's songs in the same way it
does for conventional poetry. In traditional poems,
ambiguity is very common, but there the different levels of
meaning which can be found all support one another,
thereby heightening the richness and intricacy of the
poetry. As illustrated by the line, "I'd love to turn you on,"
Beatles' lyrics often imply meanings which conflict with
one another. At the same time—and here is a strange
business—this conflict is not experienced by listeners as
the flaw that textbooks would have it to be, but rather as
the source of the Beatles' greatest poetic appeal
(excluding compositions by George Harrison). Why is this
so? For one thing, perhaps, conflict of possible meanings
in Lennon's lyrics does not lead to the sort of hopeless
confusion it produces in amateur writing. Lennon always
appears to be making sense; in fact, his words flow in such
an easy way that they almost seem to be the response of
banality to the obvious. Furthermore, after we begin
puzzling over them, they point not every whichway, but in
two clear though incompatible directions, one being
toward the celebration, the other toward the mockery of
life, and the tension between these poles is vitally
interesting.

A second feature of this special ambiguity in the Beatles' lyrics is the freedom which the ambiguity extends to the listener. This freedom is openly offered. By means of signs in the performance as well as in the content of the songs, the Beatles say in effect, "Take us how you will, and good luck to you all." In bad writing freedom of interpretation is unwanted by the audience, ungranted by the author, and issued only by mistake. Receiving it from the Beatles, listeners appreciate the honesty of the offer even—and perhaps especially—when they suspect the Beatles are thereby teasing them. More important, they also enjoy the opportunity to create their own interpretations. Their freedom is not license, of course. *A Day in the Life* cannot be interpreted as a recipe for goulash or a sermon on profanity. Lennon and McCartney should rather be regarded as inviting their audience to play an open-ended game in which each listener is left to create, within limits, his own meanings. We should also point out that one of these limits is a bar against dogmatic certainty. No listener can say that the meaning he finds is the only possible one. Always he is made aware that others may see a Beatles song in quite another light. Philosophically, this open relation of poet to listener and of listeners to one another suggests the existentialist ideals we mentioned in discussing the perspective of the New Generation. (See 3: Tim Buckley)

Later we shall see in contemporary songwriting a tendency to push the kind of ambiguity found in the Beatles' work to extremes, even to surrealism. In doing so, songwriters increase the wonder that comes from allowing the listener to become engaged in the creative process, but there is always the danger that he may just become lost for want of a system of expectations to guide his imagination. The work of Lennon and McCartney, however, avoids this pitfall, largely because of the way its contexts structure ambiguity.

As is the case with Joni Mitchell and lyric poets generally, the basic context of John Lennon's lyrics is that set by *attitude.* Also like Joni Mitchell and other successful poets, Lennon is a writer whose attitude comes through as a tension between distance and involvement, the uniqueness of his attitude being specified by the opposition of his particular qualities of character and by the kind of subject matter he treats. Basically, Lennon deals with the disparities in daily life that preoccupy the other New Generation songwriters, but he specializes in those which are in one way or another absurd. What keeps him at a distance from them is a kind of background hostility ranging from an almost cruel cynicism to a refusal to see anything but surfaces that his wit has erased clean of human significance. What involves him with his subject matter, on the other hand, is his exuberant, youthful joy in playing with these absurdities, a joy so strong he must share it with his audience. That joy courses through McCartney's music and all aspects of the Beatles' showmanship, and its summons to the audience to join in carries, perhaps, the potential for compassion that Lennon and McCartney express only rarely, but with telling effect, as in *Eleanor Rigby* and *She's Leaving Home.*

Hostility and joy are not easily fused. Their co-existence in the Beatles' songs reflects the fundamental ambiguity of meaning that we have described, the split between the mockery and celebration of life. But there are times when hostility and joy come close to fusing. These are the moments of prankish rebelliousness when the Beatles seem like adolescents out for a bit of fun. Even then, however, we don't have simple, uninteresting horseplay, for Lennon's lyrics always make it clear that the Beatles know the score, and that they have chosen to act like pranksters *because* they know it.

How the Beatles express the attitude behind Lennon's lyrics is on the most general level a question of *manner.* The context of manner is provided by the conventions of rock 'n' roll placed in the service of an imaginative spirit that coolly defies all convention. Using the rhythms of rock, the Beatles speak first to our bodies, disposing us to receive whatever else may come as dancers in a primitive ritual. Subduing these rhythms to their imagination, they speak next to our minds, calling the tune for the consciousness released in the dance and thereby involving us both physically and mentally in the attitudes they are expressing. But it is not only the rhythms of rock that the Beatles master in their art. The mask of the rock singer; the aura of youth, wildness, and mass frenzy; the resonance of modern cities doing their frantic business—the whole rock experience works for the Beatles, establishing a context for their defiance and joy which could not possibly be conveyed by Lennon's lyrics alone. And it works especially effectively when it is held back. In *Eleanor Rigby*, rock rhythms and mood are repressed, but as a result we become aware of the subtle overtones and qualifications of feeling they can give to lyrics which might otherwise be straightforward sentiment. We would also point out that in combining the ambiguously significant gestures of the lyrics with honest, punching rock rhythms, the Beatles tip off the listener that they may be conning him but welcoming him with this fair warning to make what he will of the song they sing and the life it carries.

One more context of the Beatles' songs is the style of Lennon's lyrics. Frequently we hear people speak of how "smooth" his lyrics are. What do they have in mind? In addition to the integration of his lines and the flow of his diction, they may be referring to the fact that any unqualified, undefended sentiment or obviously "arty" effort has been polished away, that what remains is a mobile of hard, bright mirrors reflecting in ever-changing patterns the light of the beholder as well as of the creator. Such a style severely distances Lennon's material. It also lets us know that he has the animal in the rock music under easy control.

Another dimension of Lennon's style is its vividness. In the polishing process, Lennon's language is reduced to elemental idioms and diction which is so simple that it is almost trivial. But after his imagination is done playing with them, not an idiom or cliché is left undisturbed by irony or a fresh way of looking and laughing. Consider, for example, *Lucy in the Sky with Diamonds*, a fantasy which is as simple as a child's drawing. But though the fantasy is child-like, the significant thing is that it is offered to adults. How can we suspend all the years we've spent being conditioned into maturity and suddenly relish again such childish goodies as "tangerine trees," "marmalade skies," and "marshmallow pies"? To our astonishment, however, we find that Lennon and McCartney make this easy for us; McCartney, by means of music that catches us up in the vision, and Lennon, by way of invisible bridges that allow us to move freely between the worlds of the child and the adult. Lucy herself is the main bridge, functioning both as a children's good fairy and a vaguely sexual ideal just beyond our reach. More subtle links are in the details of the imagery. Associated with appeals to the child in us are wry evocations of the synthetic world of adults—Lucy's "kaleidoscope eyes," "cellophane flowers," "newspaper taxis," "plasticine porters," and "looking glass ties". There is also the odd coincidence that the capital letters in the title of the song are "LSD". The juxtaposition of all these elements almost seems to make an argument: the world is absurd; ergo, *enjoy* it. And that may be as close as we can come to formulating a motto for the Beatles' songs.

A Day in the Life

Words by John Lennon; Music by Paul McCartney
Sgt. Pepper's Lonely Hearts Club Band, Capital S-MAS 2653

I read the news today oh boy
About a lucky man who made the grade
And though the news was rather sad
Well I just had to laugh
I saw the photograph.

He blew his mind out in a car
He didn't notice that the lights had changed
A crowd of people stood and stared
They'd seen his face before
Nobody was really sure
If he was from the House of Lords.

I saw a film today oh boy
The English army had just won the war
A crowd of people turned away
But I just had to look
Having read the book.

I'd love to turn you on . . .

Woke up, fell out of bed,
Dragged a comb across my head
Found my way downstairs and drank a cup,
And looking up I noticed I was late.
Found my coat and grabbed my hat
Made the bus in seconds flat
Found my way upstairs and had a smoke,
Somebody spoke and I went into a dream . . .

I read the news today oh boy
Four thousand holes in Blackburn, Lancashire
And though the holes were rather small
They had to count them all
Now they know how many holes it takes
*   to fill the Albert Hall.*

I'd love to turn you on . . .

The Legs

Robert Graves

There was this road,
And it led up-hill,
And it led down-hill,
And round and in and out.

And the traffic was legs,
Legs from the knees down,
Coming and going,
Never pausing.

And the gutters gurgled
With the rain's overflow,
And the sticks on the pavement
Blindly tapped and tapped.

What drew the legs along
Was the never-stopping,
And the senseless, frightening
Fate of being legs.

Legs for the road,
The road for legs,
Resolutely nowhere
In both directions.

My legs at least
Were not in that rout:
On grass by the road-side
Entire I stood,

Watching the unstoppable
Legs go by
With never a stumble
Between step and step.

Though my smile was broad
The legs could not see,
Though my laugh was loud
The legs could not hear.

My head dizzied, then
I wondered suddenly,
Might I too be a walker
From the knees down?

Gently I touched my shins.
The doubt unchained them:
They had run in twenty puddles
Before I regained them.

Newsreel

C. Day-Lewis

Enter the dream-house, brothers and sisters, leaving
Your debts asleep, your history at the door:
This is the home for heroes, and this loving
Darkness a fur you can afford.

Fish in their tank electrically heated
Nose without envy the glass wall: for them
Clerk, spy, nurse, killer, prince, the great and the defeated,
Move in a mute day-dream.

Bathed in this common source, you gape incurious
At what your active hours have willed–
Sleep-walking on that silver wall, the furious
Sick shapes and pregnant fancies of your world.

There is the mayor opening the oyster season:
A society wedding: the autumn hats look swell:
An old crock's race, and a politician
In fishing-waders to prove that all is well.

Oh, look at the warplanes! Screaming hysteric treble
In the long power-dive, like gannets they fall steep.
But what are they to trouble–
These silver shadows to trouble your watery, womb-deep sleep?

See the big guns, rising, groping, erected
To plant death in your world's soft womb.
Fire-bud, smoke-blossom, iron seed projected–
Are these exotics? They will grow nearer home:

Grow nearer home–and out of the dream-house stumbling
One night into a strangling air and the flung
Rags of children and thunder of stone niagaras tumbling,
You'll know you slept too long.

For the Time Being
Fugal-Chorus
W. H. Auden

Great is Caesar: He has conquered Seven Kingdoms.
The First was the Kingdom of Abstract Idea:
Last night it was Tom, Dick and Harry; tonight it is S's with P's;
Instead of inflexions and accents
There are prepositions and word-order;
Instead of aboriginal objects excluding each other
There are specimens reiterating a type;
Instead of wood-nymphs and river-demons,
There is one unconditioned ground of Being.
Great is Caesar: God must be with Him.

Great is Caesar: He has conquered Seven Kingdoms.
The Second was the Kingdom of Natural Cause:
Last night it was Sixes and Sevens; tonight it is One and Two;
Instead of saying, "Strange are the whims of the Strong,"
We say, "Harsh is the Law but it is certain";
Instead of building temples, we build laboratories;
Instead of offering sacrifices, we perform experiments;
Instead of reciting prayers, we note pointer-readings;
Our lives are no longer erratic but efficient.
Great is Caesar: God must be with Him.

Great is Caesar: He has conquered Seven Kingdoms.
The Third was the Kingdom of Infinite Number:
Last night it was Rule-of-Thumb, tonight it is To-a-T;
Instead of Quite-a-lot, there is Exactly-so-many;
Instead of Only-a-few, there is Just-these;
Instead of saying, "You must wait until I have counted,"
We say, "Here you are. You will find this answer correct";
Instead of a nodding acquaintance with a few integers
The Transcendentals are our personal friends.
Great is Caesar: God must be with Him.

Great is Caesar: He has conquered Seven Kingdoms.
The Fourth was the Kingdom of Credit Exchange:
Last night it was Tit-for-Tat, tonight it is C.O.D.;
When we have a surplus, we need not meet someone with a deficit;
When we have a deficit, we need not meet someone with a surplus;
Instead of heavy treasures, there are paper symbols of value;
Instead of Pay at Once, there is Pay when you can;
Instead of My Neighbour, there is Our Customers;
Instead of Country Fair, there is World Market.
Great is Caesar: God must be with Him.

Great is Caesar: He has conquered Seven Kingdoms.
The Fifth was the Kingdom of Inorganic Giants:
Last night it was Heave-Ho, tonight it is Whee-Spree;
When we want anything, They make it;
When we dislike anything, They change it;
When we want to go anywhere, They carry us;
When the Barbarian invades us, They raise immovable shields;
When we invade the Barbarian, They brandish irresistible swords;
Fate is no longer a fiat of Matter, but a freedom of Mind.
Great is Caesar: God must be with Him.

Great is Caesar: He has conquered Seven Kingdoms.
The Sixth was the Kingdom of Organic Dwarfs:
Last night it was Ouch-Ouch, tonight it is Yum-Yum;
When diseases waylay us, They strike them dead;
When worries intrude on us, They throw them out;
When pain accosts us, They save us from embarrassment;
When we feel like sheep, They make us lions;
When we feel like geldings, They make us stallions;
Spirit is no longer under Flesh, but on top.
Great is Caesar: God must be with Him.

Great is Caesar: He has conquered Seven Kingdoms.
The Seventh was the Kingdom of Popular Soul:
Last night it was Order-Order, tonight it is Hear-Hear;
When he says, You are happy, we laugh;
When he says, You are wretched, we cry;
When he says, It is true, everyone believes it;
When he says, It is false, no one believes it;
When he says, This is good, this is loved;
When he says, That is bad, that is hated.
Great is Caesar: God must be with Him.

pity this busy monster, manunkind
E. E. Cummings

pity this busy monster,manunkind,

not. Progress is a comfortable disease:
your victim (death and life safely beyond)

plays with the bigness of his littleness
—electrons deify one razorblade
into a mountainrange;lenses extend

unwish through curving wherewhen till unwish
returns on its unself.
                   A world of made
is not a world of born—pity poor flesh

and trees,poor stars and stones,but never this
fine specimen of hypermagical

ultraomnipotence.   We doctors know

a hopeless case if—listen:there's a hell
of a good universe next door; let's go

Eleanor Rigby

Words by John Lennon; Music by Paul McCartney
Revolver, Capitol S*T 2576

Ah, look at all the lonely people!
Ah, look at all the lonely people!

Eleanor Rigby
Picks up the rice in the church where a wedding has been
Lives in a dream
Waits at the window
Wearing the face that she keeps in a jar by the door.
Who is it for?

All the lonely people,
Where do they all come from?
All the lonely people,
Where do they all belong?

Father McKenzie,
Writing the words of a sermon that no one will hear,
No one comes near
Look at him working,
Darning his socks in the night when there's nobody there
What does he care?

All the lonely people,
Where do they all come from?
All the lonely people,
Where do they all belong?

Ah, look at all the lonely people!
Ah, look at all the lonely people!

Eleanor Rigby,
Died in the church and was buried along with her name
Nobody came
Father McKenzie,
Wiping the dirt from his hands as he walks from the grave,
No one was saved.

All the lonely people,
Where do they all come from?
All the lonely people,
Where do they all belong?

Ah, look at all the lonely people!
Ah, look at all the lonely people!

A Coney Island of the Mind, No. 8
Lawrence Ferlinghetti

In Golden Gate Park that day
                            a man and his wife were coming along
            thru the enormous meadow
                            which was the meadow of the world
He was wearing green suspenders
                            and carrying an old beat-up flute
                                            in one hand
        while his wife had a bunch of grapes
                            which she kept handing out
                                            individually
                    to various squirrels
                                    as if each
                    were a little joke

    And then the two of them came on
                            thru the enormous meadow
    which was the meadow of the world
                            and then
            at a very still spot where the trees dreamed
        and seemed to have been waiting thru all time
                                    for them
            they sat down together on the grass
                            without looking at each other
            and ate oranges
                    without looking at each other
                                    and put the peels
            in a basket which they seemed
                            to have brought for that purpose
            without looking at each other

And then
            he took his shirt and undershirt off
        but kept his hat on
                        sideways
                        and without saying anything
            fell asleep under it
                        And his wife just sat there looking
    at the birds which flew about
        calling to each other
                    in the stilly air
    as if they were questioning existence
                        or trying to recall something forgotten

But then finally
　　　　she too lay down flat
　　　　　　　　and just lay there looking up
　　　　　　　　　　　　　　at nothing
　　　　　yet fingering the old flute
　　　　　　　　　　　which nobody played
　　　　　and finally looking over
　　　　　　　　　　at him
　　　　without any particular expression
　　　　　　　　　　　　　except a certain awful look
　　　　　of terrible depression

Let Me Tell You a Little Story
(Tune: St. James' Infirmary)
W. H. Auden

Let me tell you a little story
　　About Miss Edith Gee;
She lived in Clevedon Terrace
　　At Number 83.

She'd a slight squint in her left eye,
　　Her lips they were thin and small,
She had narrow sloping shoulders
　　And she had no bust at all.

She'd a velvet hat with trimming,
　　And a dark-grey serge costume;
She lived in Clevedon Terrace
　　In a small bed-sitting room.

She'd a purple mac for wet days,
　　A green umbrella too to take,
She'd a bicycle with shopping basket
　　And a harsh back-pedal brake.

The Church of Saint Aloysius
　　Was not so very far;
She did a lot of knitting,
　　Knitting for that Church Bazaar.

Miss Gee looked up at the starlight
　　And said: "Does anyone care
That I live in Clevedon Terrace
　　On one hundred   pounds a year?"

She dreamed a dream one evening
    That she was the Queen of France
And the Vicar of Saint Aloysius
    Asked Her Majesty to dance.

But a storm blew down the palace,
    She was biking through a field of corn,
And a bull with the face of the Vicar
    Was charging with lowered horn.

She could feel his hot breath behind her,
    He was going to overtake;
And the bicycle went slower and slower
    Because of that back-pedal brake.

Summer made the trees a picture,
    Winter made them a wreck;
She bicycled to the evening service
    With her clothes buttoned up to her neck.

She passed by the loving couples,
    She turned her head away;
She passed by the loving couples
    And they didn't ask her to stay.

Miss Gee sat down in the side-aisle,
    She heard the organ play;
And the choir it sang so sweetly
    At the ending of the day,

Miss Gee knelt down in the side-aisle,
    She knelt down on her knees;
"Lead me not into temptation
    But make me a good girl, please."

The days and nights went by her
    Like waves round a Cornish wreck;
She bicycled down to the doctor
    With her clothes buttoned up to her neck.

She bicycled down to the doctor,
    And rang the surgery bell;
"O, doctor, I've a pain inside me,
    And I don't feel very well."

Doctor Thomas looked her over,
    And then he looked some more;
Walked over to his wash-basin,
    Said, "Why didn't you come before?"

Doctor Thomas sat over his dinner,
  Though his wife was waiting to ring;
Rolling his bread into pellets,
  Said, "Cancer's a funny thing.

"Nobody knows what the cause is,
  Though some pretend they do;
It's like some hidden assassin
  Waiting to strike at you.

"Childless women get it,
  And men when they retire;
It's as if there had to be some outlet
  For their foiled creative fire."

His wife she rang for the servant,
  Said, "Don't be so morbid, dear,"
He said; "I saw Miss Gee this evening
  And she's a goner, I fear."

They took Miss Gee to the hospital,
  She lay there a total wreck,
Lay in the ward for women
  With the bedclothes right up to her neck.

They laid her on the table,
  The students began to laugh;
And Mr. Rose the surgeon
  He cut Miss Gee in half.

Mr. Rose, he turned to his students,
  Said; "Gentlemen, if you please,
We seldom see a sarcoma
  As far advanced as this."

They took her off the table,
  They wheeled away Miss Gee
Down to another department
  Where they study Anatomy.

They hung her from the ceiling,
  Yes, they hung up Miss Gee;
And a couple of Oxford Groupers
  Carefully dissected her knee.

Secretary
Ted Hughes

If I should touch her she would shriek and weeping
Crawl off to nurse the terrible wound: all
Day like a starling under the bellies of bulls
She hurries among men, ducking, peeping,

Off in a whirl at the first move of a horn.
At dusk she scuttles down the gauntlet of lust
Like a clockwork mouse. Safe home at last
She mends socks with holes, shirts that are torn,

For father and brother, and a delicate supper cooks:
Goes to bed early, shuts out with the light
Her thirty years, and lies with buttocks tight,
Hiding her lovely eyes until day break.

Acquainted with the Night
Robert Frost

I have been one acquainted with the night.
I have walked out in rain—and back in rain.
I have outwalked the furthest city light.

I have looked down the saddest city lane.
I have passed by the watchman on his beat
And dropped my eyes, unwilling to explain.

I have stood still and stopped the sound of feet
When far away an interrupted cry
Came over houses from another street,

But not to call me back or say good-bye;
And further still at an unearthly height,
One luminary clock against the sky

Proclaimed the time was neither wrong nor right.
I have been one acquainted with the night.

Lucy in the Sky with Diamonds

Words by John Lennon; Music by Paul McCartney
Sgt. Pepper's Lonely Hearts Club Band, Capital S-MAS 2653

Picture yourself in a boat on a river,
With tangerine trees and marmalade skies
Somebody calls you, you answer quite slowly,
A girl with kaleidoscope eyes.
Cellophane flowers of yellow and green,
Towering over your head,
Look for the girl with the sun in her eyes,
And she's gone.

Lucy in the sky with diamonds!
Lucy in the sky with diamonds!
Lucy in the sky with diamonds!

Follow her down to a bridge by a fountain
Where rocking horse people eat marshmallow pies,
Everyone smiles as you drift past the flowers
That grow so incredibly high.
Newspaper taxis appear on the shore,
Waiting to take you away,
Climb in the back with your head in the clouds
And you're gone.

Lucy in the sky with diamonds!
Lucy in the sky with diamonds!
Lucy in the sky with diamonds!

Picture yourself on a train in a station,
With plasticine porters with looking glass ties,
Suddenly someone is there at the turnstile,
The girl with kaleidoscope eyes.

Lucy in the sky with diamonds!
Lucy in the sky with diamonds!
Lucy in the sky with diamonds!

Love in the Asylum

Dylan Thomas

A stranger has come
To share my room in the house not right in the head,
A girl mad as birds

Bolting the night of the door with her arm her plume.
Strait in the mazed bed
She deludes the heaven-proof house with entering clouds

Yet she deludes with walking the nightmarish room,
At large as the dead,
Or rides the imagined oceans of the male wards.

She has come possessed
Who admits the delusive light through the bouncing wall,
Possessed by the skies

She sleeps in the narrow trough yet she walks the dust
Yet raves at her will
On the madhouse boards worn thin by my walking tears.

And taken by light in her arms at long and dear last
I may without fail
Suffer the first vision that set fire to the stars.

Pied Beauty

Gerard Manley Hopkins

Glory be to God for dappled things—
   For skies of couple-colour as a brinded cow;
      For rose-moles all in stipple upon trout that swim;
Fresh-firecoal chestnut-falls; finches' wings;
     Landscape plotted and pieced—fold, fallow, and plough;
     And all trades, their gear and tackle and trim.

All things counter, original, spare, strange;
   Whatever is fickle, freckled (who knows how?)
     With swift, slow; sweet, sour; adazzle, dim;
He fathers-forth whose beauty is past change:
        Praise him.

Snow

Louis MacNeice

The room was suddenly rich and the great bay-window was
Spawning snow and pink roses against it
Soundlessly collateral and incompatible:
World is suddener than we fancy it.

World is crazier and more of it than we think,
Incorrigibly plural. I peel and portion
A tangerine and spit the pips and feel
The drunkenness of things being various.

And the fire flames with a bubbling sound for world
Is more spiteful and gay than one supposes—
On the the tongue on the eyes on the ears in the palms of one's hands—
There is more than glass between the snow and the huge roses.

A Thing of Beauty

John Keats
(from *Endymion*)

A thing of beauty is a joy for ever:
Its loveliness increases; it will never
Pass into nothingness; but still will keep
A bower quiet for us, and a sleep
Full of sweet dreams, and health, and quiet breathing.
Therefore, on every morrow, are we wreathing
A flowery band to bind us to the earth,
Spite of despondence, of the inhuman dearth
Of noble natures, of the gloomy days,
Of all the unhealthy and o'er-darkened ways
Made for our searching: yes, in spite of all,
Some shape of beauty moves away the pall
From our dark spirits. Such the sun, the moon,
Trees old and young, sprouting a shady boon
For simple sheep; and such are daffodils
With the green world they live in; and clear rills
That for themselves a cooling covert make
'Gainst the hot season; the mid-forest brake,
Rich with a sprinkling of fair musk-rose blooms:
And such too is the grandeur of the dooms
We have imagined for the mighty dead;
All lovely tales that we have heard or read:
An endless fountain of immortal drink,
Pouring unto us from the heaven's brink.
Nor do we merely feel these essences
For one short hour; no, even as the trees
That whisper round a temple become soon
Dear as the temple's self, so does the moon,
The passion poesy, glories infinite,
Haunt us till they become a cheering light
Unto our souls, and bound to us so fast,
That, whether there be shine, or gloom o'ercast,
They always must be with us, or we die.

6

Bruce Cockburn

In Ottawa, a small group of young Canadian songwriters and poets show what can be done by means of restraint and simplicity. Bruce Cockburn, a leading member of the group, is represented in this section by two songs on a common theme of New Generation songwriters, the loneliness that springs from failure of communication. The first song, *Bird Without Wings,* treats this theme in terms of a personal failure in love, and does so with a delicacy that could easily be missed by an insensitive ear. Listen when he sings, "I could only feel your music one line at a time"; is there a better way to describe the special mode of losing that he is singing about? The second song, *The View from Pompous Head,* might be taken as a series of sketches drawn from a vantage point isolating the artist from his subjects, a particularly apt device since what he draws are also vantage points of isolation.

Penelope Schafer, another member of the Ottawa group, is represented here by *A Sunlight Myth,* a poem that contrasts with the themes of Cockburn's songs. On the other hand, it also complements Cockburn's work by presenting a vision of the ideal physical and spiritual communion. Paul Maurice's *Catechism* marks off the extreme from this ideal by spelling out the cruelty of alienation; and Matthew Arnold's *To Marguerite* develops in detail the revelations of loneliness which come from another sensitive perspective.

Bird Without Wings

Words and Music by Bruce Cockburn
Three's a Crowd, *Christopher's Movie Matinee*,
Dunhill S-50030

In the circle of your arms
I could have set the sun in silver
And made for you a ring so fine.
If we had grown together, Babe,
We might have made it to the sea-shore
And left this muddy river far behind.
Ah, but I couldn't find the key that would unlock these chains of mine,
And my songs were not complete enough to sing,
I could only feel your music one line at a time
And there's no chance for a bird without wings.

If only I had read
The meaning that your eyes held
As they shone like diamonds burning in the dawn.
But the raindrops in my own
Changed the colour of the sky
And I just sat and helplessly looked on.
So I'll go on worshipping my world of faded dreams
Though the church bells are of lead and will not ring,
And to those who try to tell themselves I'm more than what I seem,
I say, What good is a bird without wings?

After Great Pain a Formal Feeling Comes
Emily Dickinson

After great pain a formal feeling comes–
The nerves sit ceremonious like tombs;
The stiff Heart questions–was it He that bore?
And yesterday–or centuries before?

The feet mechanical
Go round a wooden way
Of ground or air or Ought, regardless grown,
A quartz contentment like a stone.

This is the hour of lead
Remembered if outlived,
As freezing persons recollect the snow–
First chill, then stupor, then the letting go.

A Sunlight Myth
Penelope Schafer

To lose, save, my own soft skin
I lurked inside a heavy head
Confused with holy visions.
(Honey-liquid your eyes tasted.)

Our ribs melted as we exchanged
Bodies and I remember the room
Where silence was worshipped
And frankincense tasted like ginger.

We bathed in the morning
Puerto Rican oils embedded
Our souls open and bleeding
A healed spirit floated in water.

On his right shoulder the jew
Fostered a dove to sing
His sad song of love . . .
He hovered and was gone;

Leaving us alone to face the sun.
He spoke Hebrew laments
    and caressed
My lean body with unnatural insight
Where wisdom fell on naked feet.

I began to weave a golden cloak,
Inside, crescent shaped pockets
Were filled, with velvet stitched
Lessons of love you taught
To bless my barren body.

The View from Pompous Head

Words and Music by Bruce Cockburn
Three's a Crowd, *Christopher's Movie Matinee*,
Dunhill S-50030

In a brown-stone factory
My friend Jervis Fragrance sits alone
Among his reveries
Of sitting once upon a throne,
Or maybe being Prime Minister some day.
Who knows where he's wonder'd to today.

To the park day after day
His daughter Marj'rie comes to eat the lunch she packs
To save her pay
And gathers tulips in a bunch
To brighten up the office for a while.
Maybe she can get someone to smile.

Meanwhile inside city hall
The amateurs are fighting all the time
About such things as protocol
And weighty matters like the lime-stone quarry
Should it be thought of as a mine?
While small boys throw pebbles at the sign.

The citizens of the freak world
Hold themselves aloof from all
This comedy
And no one speaks except to call
On Dear Old Dad to ask him for a buck
And I just sit and wish them all "good luck".

To Marguerite

Matthew Arnold

Yes: in the sea of life enisled,
　With echoing straits between us thrown.
Dotting the shoreless watery wild,
　We mortal millions live *alone*.
The islands feel the enclasping flow,
And then their endless bounds they know.

But when the moon their hollows lights,
　And they are swept by balms of spring,
And in their glens, on starry nights,
　The nightingales divinely sing;
And lovely notes, from shore to shore,
Across the sounds and channels pour;

O then a longing like despair
　Is to their farthest caverns sent!
For surely once, they feel, we were
　Parts of a single continent.
Now round us spreads the watery plain—
O might our marges meet again!

Who ordered that their longing's fire
　Should be, as soon as kindled, cooled?
Who renders vain their deep desire?—
　A god, a god their severance ruled;
And bade betwixt their shores to be
The unplumbed, salt, estranging sea.

Catechism

Paul Maurice

Where is thy kindness
Hid in the heart
Where is thy cruelty
Below the belt
What doth the one hand
Holds the heart
What doth the other
Unbuckles the belt
Who sings thy song
My soul and my sex
To whom do they sing
Each to the other
Where is thy kindness
Below the belt
Where is thy cruelty
Hid in the heart

7

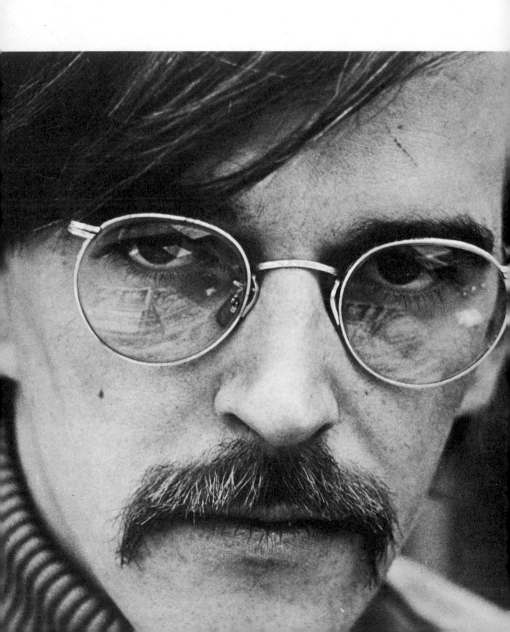

William Hawkins

Like Bruce Cockburn, William Hawkins, another writer
from Ottawa, composes both poetry and songs. His
intimate knowledge of the difference between poem and
song is reflected in the way he enables his songs to carry
poetic richness without overburdening the easy, idiomatic
style that is essential to the popular song form.

The themes of loneliness and despondency we found in
Cockburn's songs are also treated here in Hawkins'
Cotton Candy Man and *Gnostic Serenade.* Again the
dominant tone is marked by quiet restraint. In comparing
Hawkins' songs to the poems associated with them in this
section, consider especially whether Maria Nunez's poem,
Empty, proves that effective poetry can be simpler than
song, and whether Michael Drayton's poem, *Farewell to
Love,* is strengthened or marred by its air of flippant
insincerity, an attitude that Hawkins, although taking a
position similar to Drayton's, chooses to avoid.

Cotton Candy Man

Words and Music by William Hawkins
Three's a Crowd, *Christopher's Movie Matinee*,
Dunhill S-50030

It's sad when all you get is nothing
There's nobody to hold
And you're afraid you're getting old,
And you seem to be losing all the time,
A cotton candy man,
Making all the sweets he can,
But the circus never comes his way.

It's true the ladies all have their sweet things
Living in a candy land
Eating on a five-year plan
And their sweets have constant availability
They don't want a candy man,
Who isn't their ideal old man
A personable also-ran.

Nothing, that's all you get is nothing.
You're about to blow your mind
And everybody thinks it's fine
And comments on your becoming immobility,
And you lift your head and shout,
This isn't what life's all about!
This isn't what life's all about!

Empty

Maria Nuñez

No, nothing
passes
through my mind;
it is like a wide sky
empty and white.

Yet I am here,
quiet, before you,
and looking at you,
yet I do not see you.

No, nothing
passes
through my mind;
it is like a wide sky
empty and white.

Stanzas

Written in Dejection, near Naples
Percy Bysshe Shelley

The sun is warm, the sky is clear,
  The waves are dancing fast and bright,
Blue isles and snowy mountains wear
  The purple noon's transparent might,
  The breath of the moist earth is light,
Around its unexpanded buds;
  Like many a voice of one delight,
The winds, the birds, the ocean floods,
The City's voice itself, is soft like Solitude's.

I see the Deep's untrampled floor
  With green and purple seaweeds strown;
I see the waves upon the shore,
  Like light dissolved in star-showers, thrown:
  I sit upon the sands alone,–
The lightning of the noontide ocean
  Is flashing round me, and a tone
Arises from its measured motion,
How sweet! did any heart now share in my emotion.

Alas! I have nor hope nor health,
  Nor peace within nor calm around,
Nor that content surpassing wealth
  The sage in meditation found,
  And walked with inward glory crowned–
Nor fame, nor power, nor love, nor leisure.
  Others I see whom these surround–
Smiling they live, and call life pleasure:–
To me that cup has been dealt in another measure.

Yet now despair itself is mild,
  Even as the winds and waters are;
I could lie down like a tired child,
  And weep away the life of care
  Which I have borne and yet must bear,
Till death like sleep might steal on me,
  And I might feel in the warm air
My cheek grow cold, and hear the sea
Breathe o'er my dying brain its last monotony.

Some might lament that I were cold,
    As I, when this sweet day is gone,
Which my lost heart, too soon grown old,
    Insults with this untimely moan;
    They might lament–for I am one
Whom men love not,–and yet regret,
    Unlike this day, which, when the sun
Shall on its stainless glory set,
Will linger, though enjoyed, like joy in memory yet.

Gnostic Serenade

Words and Music by William Hawkins
Three's a Crowd, *Christopher's Movie Matinee*,
Dunhill S-50030

And finally we are as the times are,
We meet to part and go diff'rent ways,
And I'm trapped on this crazy star,
I've been a pris'ner all my days.

Once we were young and laughed a lot,
Happiness wasn't peculiar like today,
But I'd give you everything you think I've got
Just to prove that it needn't be this way.

Yes I know you've found another man,
And yes it was me who left you anyway,
But I'll do anything that I can
Just to convince you to stay.

Don't let tears start from your eyes,
If you can't make it, I'll find some other way,
Try to be like the stars in the sky,
Just shine on nothing and wait for the end of the day.

Farewell to Love
Michael Drayton

Since there's no help, come let us kiss and part;
Nay I have done, you get no more of me;
And I am glad, yea, glad with all my heart,
That thus so cleanly I myself can free;
Shake hands for ever, cancel all our vows,
And when we meet at any time again,
Be it not seen in either of our brows
That we one jot of former love retain.
Now at the last gasp of love's latest breath,
When his pulse failing, passion speechless lies,
When faith is kneeling by his bed of death,
And innocence is closing up his eyes,
Now if thou would'st, when all have given him over,
From death to life thou might'st him yet recover.

Thus Piteously Love Closed What He Begat
George Meredith

Thus piteously Love closed what he begat:
The union of this ever-diverse pair!
These two were rapid falcons in a snare,
Condemned to do the flitting of the bat.
Lovers beneath the singing sky of May,
They wandered once; clear as the dew on flowers:
But they fed not on the advancing hours:
Their hearts held cravings for the buried day.
Then each applied to each that fatal knife,
Deep questioning, which probes to endless dole.
Ah, what a dusty answer gets the soul
When hot for certainties in this our life!—
In tragic hints here see what evermore
Moves dark as yonder midnight ocean's force
Thundering like ramping hosts of warrior horse,
To throw that faint thin line upon the shore!

8

Jim Morrison and the Doors

In the song-poems of James Morrison, the lyricist and
lead singer for the Doors, evil seems frequently projected
as a positive good. To understand this deliberate
inversion of values, we must bear in mind the perspective
of the New Generation discussed in connection with the
work of Tim Buckley. We pointed out in that discussion the
insistence of New Generation writers on releasing what is
in effect the *being* of man and world, a task which they
feel is desperately important in a civilization that threatens
to turn all men into automata and all things into com-
modities. In the avant-garde of the New Generation,
Morrison apparently believes that the way to carry out this
task is to strike directly against all the taboos and
inhibitions which this civilization employs to blind us to
reality, to keep us "in line" and away from the distractions
of the flesh. Consequently, he and his group try to be what
William Blake called "doors of perception," which disclose
what man can really be by swinging open upon the dark,
forbidden areas of consciousness normally regarded as
the realm of sin.

Morrison is a highly controversial figure, and serious
objections can be raised against his philosophy, if not his
art. It is impossible, however, to understand the present
trends in popular songwriting without acknowledging his
influential "satanism". We should also recognize that the
issues he raises in both philosophy and art are extremely
important in established poetic tradition. This fact will
become clear when the reader turns to the poems by
Allen Tate, Irving Layton, and Walt Whitman, that follow
The End, the song in which Morrison first articulated his
astonishing vision. These poems will also serve as a rather
full commentary on Morrison's techniques and the deeper
implications of his thought. Everything will be lost,
however, if the student considers Morrison's lyrics apart
from his music, for the lyrics are only symbolic approxi-
mations of what his music works upon the mind.

The End

Music and Words by the Doors
Doors, Elektra 74007

This is the end,
Beautiful friend,
This is the end,
My only friend,
The end of our elaborate plans,
The end of everything that stands,
The end. No safety or surprise,
The end. I'll never look into your eyes
Again.

Can you picture what will be,
So limitless and free,
Desperately in need of some
     stranger's hand
In a desperate land.
Lost in a Roman wilderness of pain
And all the children are insane
All the children are insane;
Waiting for the summer rain.

There's danger on the edge of town,
Ride the king's highway.
Weird scenes inside the gold mine;
Ride the snake
Ride the snake
To the lake
The ancient lake.
The snake is long
Seven miles;
Ride the snake,
He's old and his skin is cold.

The West is the best.
The West is the best.
Get here and we'll do the rest.
The blue bus is calling us.
The blue bus is calling us.
Driver, where are you taking us?

The killer awoke before dawn,
He put his boots on,
He took a face from the ancient gallery,
And he walked on down the hall.

He went to the room where his sister lived,
And then he paid a visit to his brother,
And then he walked on down the hall.

And he came to a door.
And he looked inside
"Father?"
"Yes, son?"
"I want to kill you."
"Mother, I want to . . . "

Come on baby, take a chance with us,
Come on baby, take a chance with us,
And meet me at the back of the blue bus.

This is the end,
Beautiful friend.
This is the end,
My only friend.
It hurts to set you free
But you'll never follow me,
The end of laughter and soft lies,
The end of nights we tried to die.
This is the end.

Seasons of the Soul
II Autumn
Allen Tate

It had an autumn smell
And that was how I knew
That I was down a well:
I was no longer young;
My lips were numb and blue,
The air was like fine sand
In a butcher's stall
Or pumice to the tongue:
And when I raised my hand
I stood in the empty hall.

The round ceiling was high
And the gray light like shale
Thin, crumbling, and dry:
No rug on the bare floor
Nor any carved detail
To which the eye could glide;
I counted along the wall.
Door after closed door
Through which a shade might slide
To the cold and empty hall.

I will leave this house, I said,
There is the autumn weather—
Here, nor living nor dead;
The lights burn in the town
Where men fear together.
Then on the bare floor,
But tiptoe lest I fall,
I walked years down
Towards the front door
At the end of the empty hall.

The door was false—no key
Or lock, and I was caught
In the house; yet I could see
I had been born to it
For miles of running brought
Me back where I began.
I saw now in the wall
A door open a slit
And a fat grizzled man
Come out into the hall:

As in a moonlit street
Men meeting are too shy
To check their hurried feet
But raise their eyes and squint
As through a needle's eye
Into the faceless gloom,—
My father in a gray shawl
Gave me an unseeing glint
And entered another room!
I stood in the empty hall

And watched them come and go
From one room to another,
Old men, old women—slow,
Familiar; girls, boys;
I saw my downcast mother
Clad in her street-clothes,
Her blue eyes long and small,
Who had no look or voice
For him whose vision froze
Him in the empty hall.

A Tall Man Executes a Jig

For Malcolm Ross
Irving Layton

I
So the man spread his blanket on the field
And watched the shafts of light between the tufts
And felt the sun push the grass towards him;
The noise he heard was that of whizzing flies,
The whistlings of some small imprudent birds,
And the ambiguous rumbles of cars
That made him look up at the sky, aware
Of the gnats that tilted against the wind
And in the sunlight turned to jigging motes.
Fruitflies he'd call them except there was no fruit
About, spoiling to hatch these glitterings,
These nervous dots for which the mind supplied
The closing sentences from Thucydides,
Or from Euclid having a savage nightmare.

II
Jig jig, jig jig. Like minuscule black links
Of a chain played with by some playful
Unapparent hand or the palpitant
Summer haze bored with the hour's stillness.
He felt the sting and tingle afterwards
Of those leaving their orthodox unrest,
Leaving their undulant excitation
To drop upon his sleveless arm. The grass,
Even the wildflowers became black hairs
And himself a maddened speck among them.
Still the assaults of the small flies made him
Glad at last, until he saw purest joy
In their frantic jiggings under a hair,
So changed from those in the unrestraining air.

III
He stood up and felt himself enormous.
Felt as might Donatello over stone,
Or Plato, or as a man who has held
A loved and lovely woman in his arms
And feels his forehead touch the emptied sky
Where all antinomies flood into light.
Yet jig jig jig, the haloing black jots
Meshed with the wheeling fire of the sun:
Motion without meaning, disquietude
Without sense or purpose, ephemerides
That mottled the resting summer air till
Gusts swept them from his sight like wisps of smoke.
Yet they returned, bringing a bee who, seeing
But a tall man, left him for a marigold.

IV
He doffed his aureole of gnats and moved
Out of the field as the sun sank down,
A dying god upon the blood-red hills.
Ambition, pride, the ecstasy of sex,
And all circumstance of delight and grief,
That blood upon the mountain's side, that flood
Washed into a clear incredible pool
Below the ruddied peaks that pierced the sun.
He stood still and waited. If ever
The hour of revelation was come
It was now, here on the transfigured steep.
The sky darkened. Some birds chirped. Nothing else.
He thought the dying god had gone to sleep:
An Indian fakir on his mat of nails.

V
And on the summit of the asphalt road
Which stretched towards the fiery town, the man
Saw one hill raised like a hairy arm, dark
With pines and cedars against the stricken sun
—The arm of Moses or of Joshua.
He dropped his head and let fall the halo
Of mountains, purpling and silent as time,
To see temptation coiled before his feet:
A violated grass snake that lugged
Its intestine like a small red valise.
A cold-eyed skinflint it now was, and not
The manifest of that joyful wisdom,
The mirth and arrogant green flame of life;
Or earth's vivid tongue that flicked in praise of earth.

VI

And the man wept because pity was useless.
"Your jig's up; the flies come like kites," he said
And watched the grass snake crawl towards the hedge,
Convulsing and dragging into the dark
The satchel filled with curses for the earth,
For the odours of warm sedge, and the sun,
A blood-red organ in the dying sky.
Backwards it fell into a grassy ditch
Exposing its underside, white as milk,
And mocked by wisps of hay between its jaws;
And then it stiffened to its final length.
But though it opened its thin mouth to scream
A last silent scream that shook the black sky,
Adamant and fierce, the tall man did not curse.

VII

Beside the rigid snake the man stretched out
In fellowship of death; he lay silent
And stiff in the heavy grass with eyes shut,
Inhaling the moist odours of the night
Through which his mind tunnelled with flicking tongue
Backwards to caves, mounds, and sunken ledges
And desolate cliffs where come only kites,
And where of perished badgers and racoons
The claws alone remain, gripping the earth.
Meanwhile the green snake crept upon the sky,
Huge, his mailed coat glittering with stars that made
The night bright, and blowing thin wreaths of cloud
Athwart the moon; and as the weary man
Stood up, coiled above his head, transforming all.

Native Moments

Walt Whitman

Native moments—when you come upon me—ah you are here now,
Give me now libidinous joys only,
Give me the drench of my passions, give me life coarse and rank,
To-day I go consort with Nature's darlings, to-night too,
I am for those who believe in loose delights,
    I share the midnight orgies of young men,
I dance with the dancers and drink with the drinkers,
The echoes ring with our indecent calls,
    I pick out some low person for my dearest friend,
He shall be lawless, rude, illiterate,
    he shall be one condemned by others for deeds done,
I will play a part no longer,
    why should I exile myself from my companions?
O you shunn'd persons, I at least do not shun you,
I come forthwith in your midst, I will be your poet,
I will be more to you than to any of the rest.

Darest Thou Now O Soul

Walt Whitman

Darest thou now O soul,
Walk out with me toward the unknown region,
Where neither ground is for the feet nor any path to follow?

No map there, nor guide,
Nor voice sounding, nor touch of human hand,
Nor face with blooming flesh, nor lips, nor eyes, are in that land.

I know it not O soul,
Nor dost thou, all is a blank before us,
All waits undream'd of in that region, that inaccessible land.

Till when the ties loosen,
All but the ties eternal, Time and Space,
Nor darkness, gravitation, sense, nor any bounds bounding us.

Then we burst forth, we float,
In Time and Space O soul, prepared for them,
Equal, equipt at last, (O joy! O fruit of all!) them to fulfil O soul.

9

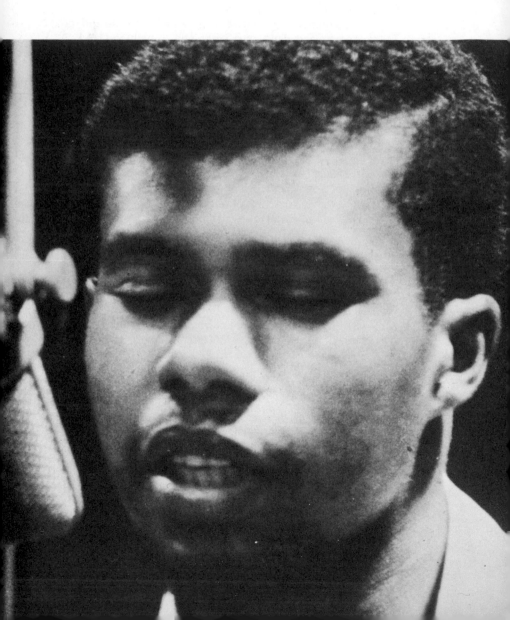

Jerry Moore

Earlier we spoke of our concern with "authentic" popular
song, song that does "justice" to ordinary life. In this
section, the songs of Jerry Moore clearly illustrate what
we mean. There is no attempt in these songs to gloss over
the problems we face in trying to "make it" in today's
world. On the contrary, Moore calls upon us to look at our
troubles squarely and to fashion a philosophy of life that
respects the facts.

In taking this approach, Moore, like other New Generation
songwriters, insists on apprehending the full reality of
what is happening around them. The *Ballad of Birmingham*
demonstrates how far this demand for truth can go.
Without making any concessions to our desire for comfort,
Dudley Randall, the distinguished American poet who
wrote the lyrics, shows us the agony of a mother whose
daughter was one of the four little girls killed in the
bombing of a Negro church in Birmingham, Alabama,
September 15, 1963. Nor has Jerry Moore mitigated the
horror by the "children's song" music he provides for
Randall's lyrics, for the resulting contrast only heightens
the impact of the story.

In *Life Is a Constant Journey Home,* Jerry Moore deals
with reality in more general terms. Of special interest is the
fact that the kind of escapism Moore attacks in this song
is not the obvious sort peddled in the marketplace, but
rather the genuinely fascinating temptations of contem-
porary psychedelic philosophy. Moore tacitly recognizes
the arguments that can be made in its favor as an
exploration of a higher or "inner" reality. In other words,
for him the question is not so much a matter of reality
versus escapism as it is the choice of the correct under-
standing of reality. In the days of tin pan alley, no one
would dream that such a subtle issue could arise in
popular song.

But is there only one correct understanding of reality?
Some academics may think so, but a man can feel justified

in taking a number of different attitudes toward the same set of facts. Thus Jerry Moore shifts from the sceptical, bitter view of life expressed in the preceding song to an affirmation of it in *This Is My Time.* We still feel he is looking at the same world, however, because *This Is My Time* affirms life in full recognition of the evils alluded to in *Life Is a Constant Journey Home.*

Special to the New York Times by Claude Sitton
BIRMINGHAM, Ala., Sept. 15—A bomb severely damaged a Negro church today during Sunday School services, killing four Negro girls and setting off racial rioting and other violence in which two Negro boys were shot to death. . . . None of the 50 bombings of Negro property here since World War II have been solved. . . . The four girls killed in the blast had just heard Mrs. Ella C. Demand, their teacher, complete the Sunday School lesson for the day. The subject was "The Love That Forgives". . . . Church members said they found the girls huddled together beneath a pile of masonry debris.

Both parents of each of three of the victims teach in the city's schools. The dead were identified by University Hospital officials as: Cynthia Wesley, 14, the only child of Claude A. Wesley, principal of the Lewis Elementary School, and Mrs. Wesley, a teacher there; Denise McNair, 11, also an only child, whose parents are teachers; Carol Robertson, 14, whose parents are teachers and whose grandmother, Mrs. Sallie Anderson, is one of the Negro members of a bi-racial committee established by Mayor Boutwell to deal with racial problems; Addie MacCollins, 14, about whom no information was immediately available.

Special to the New York Times by John Herbers
BIRMINGHAM, Ala., Sept. 15—The stained glass windows of the 16th Street Baptist Church were blown out of their frames in today's explosion. The one remaining window, which was damaged, showed Jesus leading little children . . . .

After the explosion, scores of young Negroes who had been attending Sunday School began pouring out of the entrances. Some were bleeding, some were moaning. Negro bystanders sobbed and prayed as the bodies of four dead girls were brought out of the debris.

"Oh God," a boy said. "She's my sister. She's dead."

A teen-age Negro boy knelt in the street and said the Lord's Prayer. Negro residents from blocks around began to pour out of their homes and rush to the scene in anger.

Ballad of Birmingham

Words by Dudley Randall; Music by Jerry Moore
Jerry Moore, ESP Disk 1061

Mother dear may I go downtown
Instead of out to play
And march the streets of Birmingham
In a freedom march today?

No baby no, you may not go
For the dogs are fierce and wild,
And clubs and hoses, guns and jails
Aren't good for a little child.

But mother I won't be alone,
Other children will go with me
And march the streets of Birmingham
To make our people free.

No baby no, you may not go
I fear the guns will fire,
But you may go to church instead and sing in the
  children's choir.

She's combed and brushed her night dark hair
And bathed rose petal sweet,
And drawn white gloves on small brown hands,
White shoes on her feet.

Her mother smiled to know her child
Was in that sacred place,
But that smile was the last
Smile to come to her face.

For when she heard the explosion
Her eyes grew wet and wild,
She raced through the streets of Birmingham
Yelling for her child.

She dug in bits of glass and brick,
Then pulled out a shoe–
Oh here is the shoe my baby wore
But baby where are you?

Birmingham Sunday

(September 15, 1963)
Langston Hughes

Four little girls
Who went to Sunday School that day
And never came back home at all
But left instead
Their blood upon the wall
With spattered flesh
And bloodied Sunday dresses
Torn to shreds by dynamite
That China made aeons ago—
Did not know
That what China made
Before China was ever Red at all
Would redden with their blood
This Birmingham-on-Sunday wall.

Four tiny girls
Who left their blood upon that wall,
In little graves today await
The dynamite that might ignite
The fuse of centuries of Dragon Kings
Whose tomorrow sings a hymn
The missionaries never taught Chinese
In Christian Sunday School
To implement the Golden Rule.

Four little girls
Might be awakened someday soon
By songs upon the breeze
As yet unfelt among magnolia trees.

Puzzled

Langston Hughes

Here on the edge of hell
Stands Harlem—
Remembering the old lies,
The old kicks in the back,
The old, *Be patient,*
They told us before.

Sure, we remember.
Now, when the man at the corner store
Says sugar's gone up another two cents,
And bread one,
And there's a new tax on cigarettes—
We remember the job we never had,
Never could get,
And can't have now
Because we're colored.

So we stand here
On the edge of hell
In Harlem
And look out on the world
And wonder
What we're gonna do
In the face of
What we remember.

Benediction

Bob Kaufman

Pale brown Moses went down to Egypt land
To let somebody's people go.
Keep him out of Florida, no UN there:
The poor governor is all one,
With six hundred thousand illiterates.

America, I forgive you . . . I forgive you
Nailing black Jesus to an imported cross
Every six weeks in Dawson, Georgia.
America, I forgive you . . . I forgive you
Eating black children, I know your hunger.
America, I forgive you . . . I forgive you
Burning Japanese babies defensively—
I realize how necessary it was.
Your ancestor had beautiful thoughts in his brain.
His descendants are experts in real estate.
Your generals have mushrooming visions.
Every day your people get more and more
Cars, televisions, sickness, death dreams.
You must have been great
Alive.

Life Is a Constant Journey Home
Words and Music by Jerry Moore
Jerry Moore, ESP Disk 1061

*Life is a constant journey home and sometimes I think if I could
    be back where I started I'd be where I'm going.
But I've no time for the fun of philosophying
The reality of suffering is more fact before my eyes than
    realities to be perceived only with the inner eye.*

*Well the sun is but a hole up in the sky and on the other side
    where light comes through if you've a mind to you can fly.
I say, woman, woman, how do you know my name—a name my mother
    never told me I had.
Don't tempt me to wander in pastures of fantasy
Troubled minds turn too easily their faces from reality.*

*Round round the cycles of life
With all its joys and bliss it seems too well I've known the strife.
Who cursed me before I was born
Who wished me misery as I lay at rest in the warmth of my
    mother's tender breast.
Well life is a constant journey home.
And sometimes I think if I could be back where it started I'd
    be where I'm going.*

Prayer Before Birth
Louis MacNeice

I am not yet born; O hear me.
Let not the bloodsucking bat or the rat or the stoat or the
     clubfooted ghoul come near me.

I am not yet born; console me.
I fear that the human race may with tall walls wall me,
     with strong drugs dope me, with wise lies lure me,
          on black racks rack me, in blood-baths roll me.

I am not yet born; provide me
With water to dandle me, grass to grow for me, trees to talk
     to me, sky to sing to me, birds and a white light
          in the back of my mind to guide me.

I am not yet born; forgive me
For the sins that in me the world shall commit, my words
     when they speak me, my thoughts when they think me,
          my treason engendered by traitors beyond me,
               my life when they murder by means of my
                    hands, my death when they live me.

I am not yet born; rehearse me
In the parts I must play and the cues I must take when
     old men lecture me, bureaucrats hector me, mountains
          frown at me, lovers laugh at me, the white
               waves call me to folly and the desert calls
                    me to doom and the beggar refuses
                         my gift and my children curse me.

I am not yet born; O hear me,
Let not the man who is beast or who thinks he is God
     come near me.

I am not yet born; O fill me
With strength against those who would freeze my
     humanity, would dragoon me into a lethal automaton,
          would make me a cog in a machine, a thing with
               one face, a thing, and against all those
                    who would dissipate my entirety, would
                         blow me like thistledown hither and
                              thither or hither and thither
                                   like water held in the
                                        hands would spill me
Let them not make me a stone and let them not spill me.
Otherwise kill me.

Man

Henry Vaughan
(from *Silex Scintillans*)

Weighing the steadfastness and state
Of some mean things which here below reside,
Where birds like watchful clocks the noiseless date
    And intercourse of times divide,
Where bees at night get home and hive, and flowers
    Early, as well as late,
Rise with the sun, and set in the same bowers;

I would, said I, my God would give
The staidness of these things to man! for these
To his divine appointments ever cleave,
    And no new business breaks their peace;
The birds nor sow nor reap, yet sup and dine,
    The flowers without clothes live,
Yet Solomon was never dressed so fine.

Man hath still either toys or care,
He hath no root, nor to one place is tied,
But ever restless and irregular
    About this earth doth run and ride;
He knows he hath a home, but scarce knows where,
    He says it is so far
That he hath quite forgot how to go there.

He knocks at all the doors, strays and roams,
Nay, hath not so much wit as some stones have,
Which in the darkest nights point to their homes
    By some hid sense their maker gave;
Man is the shuttle, to whose winding quest
    And passage through these looms
God ordered motion, but ordained no rest.

This Is My Time

Words and Music by Jerry Moore
Jerry Moore, ESP Disk 1061

This is my time
Tomorrow ain't yet
This is the moment of truth
When the whole human race is making the bet
That in the shadow of megaton atoms her children will grow
Higher than any ole' mushroom cloud
To find the morning rainbow.

This is my time
Restless and wild
This is the new renaissance of creative thinking and curious styles
And mini-skirt mamas who
Shake it and take it and leave you to whine
Or give you a love that is so flipped out and tripped out
*   it's bound to blow your mind.*

Oh the prophets say we're living in the time of the end
But the atom child is living
Like he's trying to catch the wind.
Up wind of tomorrow—perhaps they will see
Just what it was that made us the way we happen to be.

Perhaps they'll discover these words on my wall
This is my time
Be it damned or divine
I am a part of it all.

Strange Hurt
Langston Hughes

In times of stormy weather
She felt queer pain
That said,
"You'll find rain better
Than shelter from the rain."

Days filled with fiery sunshine
Strange hurt she knew
That made
Her seek the burning sunlight
Rather than the shade.

In months of snowy winter
When cozy houses hold,
She'd break down doors
To wander naked
In the cold.

Five Ways to Kill a Man
Edwin Brock

There are many cumbersome ways to kill a man:
you can make him carry a plank of wood
to the top of a hill and nail him to it. To do this
properly you require a crowd of people
wearing sandals, a cock that crows, a cloak
to dissect, a sponge, some vinegar and one
man to hammer the nails home.

Or you can take a length of steel,
shaped and chased in a traditional way,
and attempt to pierce the metal cage he wears.
But for this you need white horses,
English trees, men with bows and arrows,
at least two flags, a prince and a
castle to hold your banquet in.

Dispensing with nobility, you may, if the wind
allows, blow gas at him. But then you need
a mile of mud sliced through with ditches,
not to mention black boots, bomb craters,
more mud, a plague of rats, a dozen songs
and some round hats made of steel.

In an age of aeroplanes, you may fly
miles above your victim and dispose of him by
pressing one small switch. All you then
require is an ocean to separate you, two
systems of government, a nation's scientists,
several factories, a psychopath and
land that no one needs for several years.

These are, as I began, cumbersome ways
to kill a man. Simpler, direct, and much more neat
is to see that he is living somewhere in the middle
of the twentieth century, and leave him there.

Next, Please

Philip Larkin

Always too eager for the future, we
Pick up bad habits of expectancy.
Something is always approaching; every day
Till then we say,

Watching from a bluff the tiny, clear,
Sparkling armada of promises draw near.
How slow they are! And how much time they waste,
Refusing to make haste!

Yet still they leave us holding wretched stalks
Of disappointment, for, though nothing balks
Each big approach, leaning with brasswork prinked,
Each rope distinct,

Flagged, and the figurehead with golden tits
Arching our way, it never anchors; it's
No sooner present than it turns to past.
Right to the last

We think each one will heave to and unload
All good into our lives, all we are owed
For waiting so devoutly and so long.
But we are wrong:

Only one ship is seeking us, a black-
Sailed unfamiliar, towing at her back
A huge and birdless silence. In her wake
No waters breed or break.

The Passionate Man's Pilgrimage

Sir Walter Ralegh

Give me my scallop-shell of quiet,
My staff of faith to walk upon,
My scrip of joy, immortal diet,
My bottle of salvation,
My gown of glory, hope's true gage,
And thus I'll take my pilgrimage.

Blood must be my body's balmer,
No other balm will there be given,
Whilst my soul like a white palmer
Travels to the land of heaven,
Over the silver mountains,
Where spring the nectar fountains;
And there I'll kiss
The bowl of bliss,
And drink my eternal fill
On every milken hill.
My soul will be a-dry before,
But after it will ne'er thirst more;

And by the happy blissful way
More peaceful pilgrims I shall see,
That have shook off their gowns of clay
And go appareled fresh like me.
I'll bring them first
To slake their thirst,
And then to taste those nectar suckets,
At the clear wells
Where sweetness dwells,
Drawn up by saints in crystal buckets.

And when our bottles and all we
Are filled with immortality,
Then the holy paths we'll travel,
Strewed with rubies thick as gravel,
Ceilings of diamonds, sapphire floors,
High walls of coral, and pearl bowers.

From thence to heaven's bribeless hall
Where no corrupted voices brawl,
No conscience molten into gold,
Nor forged accusers bought and sold,
No cause deferred, nor vain-spent journey,
For there Christ is the king's attorney,
Who pleads for all without degrees,
And he hath angels, but no fees.
When the grand twelve million jury
Of our sins and sinful fury,
'Gainst our souls black verdicts give,
Christ pleads his death, and then we live.
Be thou my speaker, taintless pleader,
Unblotted lawyer, true proceeder,
Thou movest salvation even for alms,
Not with a bribèd lawyer's palms.

And this is my eternal plea
To him that made heaven, earth, and sea,
Seeing my flesh must die so soon,
And want a head to dine next noon,
Just at the stroke when my veins
        start and spread,
Set on my soul an everlasting head.

Then am I ready, like a palmer fit,
To tread those blest paths
        which before I writ.

10

United States of America

In this section, the songs of the rock group, The United States of America, illustrate the flexibility of the rock idiom. Though not to be judged as important poetry, the lyrics of these songs bear the marks of poetic seriousness and indicate what might come in the future of rock. *The American Metaphysical Circus,* for example, is a highly symbolic commentary on debasement and commercialism in modern society. One can see how close this song approaches the realms of genuine poetic reflectiveness by comparing it to the poems of Bob Kaufman, Karl Shapiro, and Louis MacNeice which treat these same themes. Consider also the truth and pathos of *Stranded in Time* and the detailed development of a single image in *The Garden of Earthly Delights.*

The American Metaphysical Circus

Words and Music by Joseph Byrd
United States of America, Columbia CS 9614

At precisely eight-o-five
Doctor Frederick von Meier
Will attempt his famous dive
Through a solid sheet of luminescent fire.

In the center of the ring
They are torturing a bear
And although he cannot sing
They can make him whistle Londonderry Air.

And the price is right,
The cost of one admission is your mind.

We shall shortly institute
A synopticon of fear
While it's painful, it will suit
Many customers whose appetites are queer.

Or for those who wish to pay
There are children you can bleed
In a most peculiar way
We can give you all the instruments you'll need.

And the price is right,
The cost of one admission is your mind.

If you're harder yet to serve
We have most delightful dreams;
Our recorders will preserve
The intensity and passion of your screams.

For we only aim to please;
It's our customers who gain.
As their appetites increase
They must come to us for pleasure and for pain.

And the price is right,
The cost of one admission is your mind.

Plea

Bob Kaufman

Voyager, wanderer of the heart,
Off to
    a million midnights, black, black,
Voyager, wanderer of star worlds,
Off to
    a million tomorrows, black, black,
Seek and find Hiroshima's children,
    Send them back, send them back.
Tear open concrete-sealed cathedrals, spiritually locked,
    Fill vacant theaters with their musty diversions,
    Almost forgotten laughter.

Give us back the twisted sons
Poisoned by mildewed fathers.
Find again the used-up whores,
Dying in some forgotten corner,
Find sunlight, and barking dogs,
For the lost, decayed in sorry jails.
Find pity, find Hell for wax bitches,
Hidden in the bowels of male Cadillacs.
Find tomorrow and nexttime for Negro millionaires
Hopelessly trapped in their luxurious complexions.
Find love, and an everlasting fix for hopeless junkies,
Stealing into lost night, long time.

Voyager now,
    Off to a million midnights, black, black,
Seek and find Hiroshima's children,
    Send them back, send them back.

Bagpipe Music

Louis MacNeice

It's no go the merrygoround, it's no go the rickshaw,
All we want is a limousine and a ticket for the peepshow.
Their knickers are made of crepe-de-chine, their shoes are made
        of python,
Their halls are lined with tiger rugs and their walls with
        heads of bison.

John MacDonald found a corpse, put it under the sofa,
Waited till it came to life and hit it with a poker,
Sold its eyes for souvenirs, sold its blood for whiskey,
Kept its bones for dumb-bells to use when he was fifty.
It's no go the Yogi-Man, it's no go Blavatsky,
All we want is a bank balance and a bit of skirt in a taxi.

Annie MacDougall went to milk, caught her foot in the heather,
Woke to hear a dance record playing of Old Vienna.
It's no go your maidenheads, it's no go your culture,
All we want is a Dunlop tyre and the devil mend the puncture.

The Laird o' Phelps spent Hogmanay declaring he was sober,
Counted his feet to prove the fact and found he had only
        one foot over.
Mrs. Carmichael had her fifth, looked at the job with repulsion,
Said to the midwife "Take it away; I'm through with
        over-production."

It's no go the gossip column, it's no go the Ceilidh,
All we want is a mother's help and a sugar-stick for the baby.

Willie Murray cut his thumb, couldn't count the damage,
Took the hide of an Ayrshire cow and used it for a bandage.
His brother caught three hundred cran when the seas were lavish,
Threw the bleeders back in the sea and went upon the parish.

It's no go the Herring Board, it's no go the Bible,
All we want is a packet of fags when our hands are idle.

It's no go the picture palace, it's no go the stadium,
It's no go the country cot with a pot of pink geraniums.
It's no go the Government grants, it's no go the elections,
Sit on your arse for fifty years and hang your hat on a pension.
It's no go my honey love, it's no go my poppet;
Work your hands from day to day, the winds will blow the profit.
The glass is falling hour by hour, the glass will fall for ever,
But if you break the bloody glass you won't hold up the weather.

Drug Store

I do remember an apothecary,
And hereabouts 'a dwells
Karl Shapiro

It baffles the foreigner like an idiom,
And he is right to adopt it as a form
Less serious than the living-room or bar;
    For it disestablishes the café,
Is a collective, and on basic country.

Not that it praises hygiene and corrupts
The ice-cream parlor and the tobacconist's
Is it a center; but that the attractive symbols
    Watch over puberty and leer
Like rubber bottles waiting for sick-use.

Youth comes to jingle nickels and crack wise;
The baseball scores are his, the magazines
Devoted to lust, the jazz, the Coca-Cola,
    The lending-library of love's latest.
He is the customer; he is heroized.

And every nook and cranny of the flesh
Is spoken to by packages with wiles.
"Buy me, buy me," they whimper and cajole;
    The hectic range of lipstick pouts,
Revealing the wicked and the simple mouth.

With scarcely any evasion in their eye
They smoke, undress their girls, exact a stance;
But only for a moment. The clock goes round;
    Crude fellowships are made and lost;
They slump in booths like rags, not even drunk.

A Coney Island of the Mind, No. 17
Lawrence Ferlinghetti

This life is not a circus where
the shy performing dogs of love
                              look on
as time flicks out
                    its tricky whip
                              to race us thru our paces
Yet gay parading floats drift by
                    decorated with gorgeous gussies in silk tights
                        and attended by moithering monkeys
                              make-believe monks
                              horny hiawathas
                    and baboons astride tame tigers
                        with ladies inside
            while googly horns make merrygoround music
        and pantomimic pierrots castrate disaster
            with strange sad laughter
        and gory gorillas toss tender maidens heavenward
            while cakewalkers and carnie hustlers
                all gassed to the gills
                    strike playbill poses
                and stagger after every
                              wheeling thing
        While still around the ring
                        lope the misshapen camels of lust
        and all us Emmett Kelly clowns
                        always making up imaginary scenes
with all our masks for faces
                    even eat fake Last Suppers
                              at collapsible tables
            and mocking cross ourselves
                        in sawdust crosses

And yet gobble up at last
                    to shrive our circus souls
            the also imaginary
                        wafers of grace

Finis Carnivalis

Linda Marshall

The ride has taken its course
Merry-go-rounds grind to a halt
Loudspeaking music gives up the ghost
The tickets are worth no entrance.
Cupie dolls cover their breasts with a giggle
The freaks are drinking coffee in big and little cups
Tents sigh out their air swooping to rest
And there is no more carnival.

The bearded lady fingers her Gillette
Dreaming of lilies; three-breasted Martha
Considers her pound of flesh as
The love-boats cut the last dark channels
Where obscenities whisper names.
Androgyne makes love to his shadow
Fish-maiden cleans her tank
And there is no more carnival.

Lights are disconnected everywhere
Deepening the fun house hysteric gloom
The familiar bone man collects his scythe
To spear the litter from the ground
Someone has thrown up on the ferris wheel
And the last rockets of the apocalypse
Rip the night with a curse and die
And there is no more carnival.

Stranded in Time

Words and music by Gordon Marron and Ed Bogas
United States of America, Columbia CS 9614

Early in the morning
When the sun is still asleep,
Father drinks his cup of coffee,
Kisses Mother on the cheek,
Off to work he goes
What he does nobody knows
But he's sure to bring home money every week.

Time when he and Mother were young,
Now those days are departed,
Now he's left brokenhearted,
Stranded in time.

They dote upon the children
Like some characters in plays
As if nearness to their youngers
Would recall their golden days.

And Father sold the looking glass
That once stood in the hall
And now Mother tends to tell the time
By pictures on the wall.

Times when she would laugh in his arms
Are now vanished forever,
Now they stand close together,
Stranded in time.

Les Sylphides
Louis MacNeice

Life in a day: he took his girl to the ballet;
Being shortsighted himself could hardly see it–
 The white skirts in the grey
 Glade and the swell of the music
 Lifting the white sails.

Calyx upon calyx, canterbury bells in the breeze
The flowers on the left mirror to the flowers on the right
 And the naked arms above
 The powdered faces moving
 Like seaweed in a pool.

Now, he thought, we are floating–ageless, oarless–
Now there is no separation, from now on
 You will be wearing white
 Satin and a red sash
 Under the waltzing trees.

But the music stopped, the dancers took their curtain,
The river had come to a lock–a shuffle of programmes–
 And we cannot continue down
 Stream unless we are ready
 To enter the lock and drop.

So they were married–to be the more together–
And found they were never again so much together,
 Divided by the morning tea,
 By the evening paper,
 By children and tradesmen's bills.

Waking at times in the night she found assurance
In his regular breathing but wondered whether
 It was really worth it and where
 The river had flowed away
 And where were the white flowers.

Talking in Bed
Philip Larkin

Talking in bed ought to be easiest,
Lying together there goes back so far,
An emblem of two people being honest.

Yet more and more time passes silently.
Outside, the wind's incomplete unrest
Builds and disperses clouds about the sky,

And dark towns heap up on the horizon.
None of this cares for us. Nothing shows why
At this unique distance from isolation

It becomes still more difficult to find
Words at once true and kind,
Or not untrue and not unkind.

That Time of Year Thou Mayst in Me Behold
William Shakespeare

That time of year thou mayst in me behold
When yellow leaves, or none, or few, do hang
Upon those boughs which shake against the cold,
Bare ruined choirs where late the sweet birds sang.
In me thou see'st the twilight of such day
As after sunset fadeth in the west,
Which by and by black night doth take away,
Death's second self, that seals up all in rest.
In me thou see'st the glowing of such fire,
That on the ashes of his youth doth lie
As the deathbed whereon it must expire,
Consumed with that which it was nourished by.
    This thou perceivest, which makes thy love more strong,
    To love that well which thou must leave ere long.

A Modest Proposal

Ted Hughes

There is no better way to know us
Than as two wolves, come separately to a wood.
Now neither's able to sleep–even at a distance
Distracted by the soft competing pulse
Of the other; nor able to hunt–at every step
Looking backwards and sideways, warying to listen
For the other's slavering rush. Neither can make die
The painful burning of the coal in its heart
Till the other's body and the whole wood is its own.
Then it might sob contentment toward the moon.

Each in a thicket, rage hoarse in its labouring
Chest after a skirmish, licks the rents in its hide,
Eyes brighter than is natural under the leaves
(Where the wren, peeping round a leaf, shrieks out
To see a chink so terrifyingly open
Onto the red smelting of hatred) as each
Pictures a mad final satisfaction.

Suddenly they duck and peer.
                          And there rides by
The great lord from hunting. His embroidered
Cloak floats, the tail of his horse pours,
And at his stirrup the two great-eyed greyhounds
That day after day bring down the towering stag
Leap like one, making delighted sounds.   *

The Garden of Earthly Delights

Music by Joseph Byrd;
Words by Dorothy Moskowitz
and Joseph Byrd
United States of America, Columbia CS 9614

Poisonous gardens, lethal and sweet,
Venomous blossoms
Choleric fruit, deadly to eat.

Violet nightshades, innocent bloom,
Omnivorous orchids,
Cautiously wait, hungrily loom.

>   *You will find them in her eyes,*
>   *In her eyes, In her eyes.*

Petrified willows, twisted and brown
Carrion swallows,
Wait in the wet darkening ground.

Withering shadows, quietly grow,
Potently breeding
Into a spectacular glow.

>   *You will find them in her eyes,*
>   *In her eyes, In her eyes.*

Lemonous petals, dissident play,
Tasting of ergot,
Dancing by night, dying by day.

Blackening mushrooms drink in the rain,
Sinister nightblooms
Wilt with the dawn's welcoming pain.

>   *You will find them in her eyes,*
>   *In her eyes, In her eyes.*

An Evil Spirit, Your Beauty, Haunts Me Still
Michael Drayton

An evil spirit, your beauty, haunts me still,
Wherewith, alas, I have been long possessed,
Which ceaseth not to tempt me to each ill,
Nor gives me once but one poor minute's rest;
In me it speaks, whether I sleep or wake,
And when by means to drive it out I try,
With greater torments then it me doth take,
And tortures me in most extremity;
Before my face it lays down by despairs,
And hastes me on unto a sudden death,
Now tempting me to drown myself in tears,
And then in sighing to give up my breath.
   Thus am I still provoked to every evil
   By this good wicked spirit, sweet angel devil.

Eyes of Night-Time
Muriel Rukeyser

On the roads at night I saw the glitter of eyes:
my dark around me let shine one ray; that black
allowed their eyes: spangles in the cat's, air in the moth's eye shine,
mosaic of the fly, ruby-eyed beetle, the eyes that never weep,
the horned toad sitting and its tear of blood,
fighters and prisoners in the forest, people
aware in this almost total dark, with the difference,
the one broad fact of light.

Eyes on the road at night, sides of a road like rhyme;
the floor of the illumined shadow sea
and shallows with their assembling flash and show
of sight, root, holdfast, eyes of the brittle stars.
And your eyes in the shadowy red room,
scent of the forest entering, various time
calling and the light of wood along the ceiling
and over us birds calling and their circuit eyes.
And in our bodies the eyes of the dead and the living
giving us gifts at hand, the glitter of all their eyes.

11

Robin Williamson

What should we do with a poem or song that doesn't make sense? The answer is that we shouldn't *do* anything at all with it; rather, we should let *it* do things to us, and then see whether what happens is interesting. But there is a problem in letting poems and songs of this sort go to work on us. It is no simple matter to suspend our normal demands for rationality and for messages that point in clear directions, to be unafraid of having the deeper realms of our sensibilities invaded—and this is especially difficult for the members of a technological society who survive by virtue of their reason and defense mechanisms. Recognizing our resistance, song-poets like John Lennon lead us to the edge of this kind of responsiveness by first engaging us at the level of our rationalistic, defensive, ordinary reactions to life. The songs and poems we are referring to here, however, make few if any concessions to our normal way of processing communications. Representing what might be called "surrealist" verse, they aim immediately and directly at the nether regions of consciousness. To receive them we must exercise not effort, but *non*-effort. The trick is to drop out of the work-a-day world for a while, and to *be* instead of do.

Difficult as it may sound, this prescription is not new. For almost a hundred years now artists have required these adjustments of people who want to appreciate modern art. And for countless centuries mystics have practised the art of suspending worldly perspective in order to experience their gods. What is new is the fact that today popular songwriters are turning to the mode of the avant-garde artist and the mystic, and that young audiences are willing to undergo the liberation process necessary for listening to these experimenters. Here we present one example of the new surrealist songs— *The Mad Hatter's Song,* written by Robin Williamson of the Incredible String Band.

The Mad Hatter's Song

Words and Music by Robin Williamson
The Incredible String Band,
The 5000 Spirits, Elektra EKS 74010

Oh, seekers of spring
How could you not find contentment
In a time of riddling reason in this land of the blind?
By the joke of fate alone
It's sure that as the loved hand leaves you
You clutch for the slip-stream the realness to find.
But, do what you like, do what you like,
Do what you like, do what you like,
Do what you like, do what you can,
Do what you can, live till you die.

My poor little man,
For Jesus will stretch out his hand no more.
But in the south there's many a wave
Tree; oh, would that musky fingers move your pain;
In the warm south winds the lost flowers move again.

And if you cried you know you'd fill a lake with tears,
Still wouldn't turn back the years,
Since the city has took you Mad Hatter's on my mind
So sad,
Sad to see the way it grew
Those other people that I knew
That have either fell or faltered,
Mad Hatter's on my mind.
And you must have to see clear sometime.

Prometheus the problem child still juggling with his brains,
Gives his limping leopard's visions to the miser in his veins,
Within the ruined factory the normal soul insane,
As he sets the sky beneath his heels and learns away the pain.

But I am the archer, the lover of laughter,
And mine is the arrowed flight.
I am the archer, and my eyes yearn after
The unsullied sight,
Born of the dark waters of the daughters of night;
Dancing without movement after the clear light.

Oh, Perithian fate be kind,
In the rumbling and trundeling rickshaw of time,
Hooked by the heart to the Kingfisher's line.
I will set my one eye for the shores of the blind.

Friends & Relations (A Childish Tale)
John Harney

An old man down the street
Whenever we meet
Says I keep an idle watch;
He always answers my *why,*
But though I hear I never catch
His point. Is the sky deep or high?
Listen and you may remember.

Why not wheel around, turn about,
See the sun in God's eye
And the moon in Maizie's hair.

Mrs. Jones across the way
Lives in a covey of diapers;
They'd flurry out of her basket
And perch along her lifeline
Foretelling an early death
And a grey man who'll come to stay,
But she'll shake the breath
And nonsense out of them
And beat them into line
Into line, beat them into line.

Sure, stand on your head,
Never eat bread, or the clouds
Will hide the raffish sun.

Like mother who was never fond
Of peddlers meddling medlars,
Quinces and cream with the more
Decent sort of fruit. They'd score
The alleys with their store
Of root, stem and leaves, all
Obviously meant to appall
The ears of that tender frond,
Her son, who
Turns about, stands on his head,
Never eats bread
In deference to the stars that blew
Sunday out of fashion.

But, oh father was a sailor,
An indifferent tailor,
Mason, jack of all knaves,
A rooter, a scorer, a digger
Of other men's graves. Lost
In a certain Maizie's hair
He swung off the moon
And looked for a son in God's eye,

Who'll swing you about, spin out
A thread, fill you with dread,
Shove you in the maze's lair

To fire a sun in God's eye,
And sound the sky-high sea-deep
Quest of all riddlers.

The Cold Green Element
Irving Layton

At the end of the garden walk
the wind and its satellite wait for me;
their meaning I will not know
      until I go there,
but the black-hatted undertaker

who, passing, saw my heart beating in the grass,
is also going there. Hi, I tell him,
a great squall in the Pacific blew a dead poet
      out of the water,
who now hangs from the city's gates.

Crowds depart daily to see it, and return
with grimaces and incomprehension;
if its limbs twitched in the air
      they would sit at its feet
peeling their oranges.

And turning over I embrace like a lover
the trunk of a tree, one of those
for whom the lightning was too much
      and grew a brilliant
hunchback with a crown of leaves.

The ailments escaped from the labels
of medicine bottles are all fled to the wind;
I've seen myself lately in the eyes
        of old women,
spent streams mourning my manhood,

in whose old pupils the sun became
a bloodsmear on broad catalpa leaves
and hanging from ancient twigs,
        my murdered selves
sparked the air like the muted collisions

of fruit. A black dog howls down my blood,
a black dog with yellow eyes;
he too by someone's inadvertence
        saw the bloodsmear
on the broad catalpa leaves.

But the furies clear a path for me to the worm
who sang for an hour in the throat of a robin,
and misled by the cries of young boys
        I am again
a breathless swimmer in that cold green element.

12

Myth and The Ballad of Frankie Lee and Judas Priest

In discussing Robin Williamson's *The Mad Hatter's Song,*
we spoke of what must be done to open ourselves to
surrealist poetry and song. Bob Dylan's *Ballad of Frankie
Lee and Judas Priest* also requires inner liberation if we
are to let ourselves respond fully. But Dylan has ways of
helping us let go. There is a simple, clean line of action
allowing us to slip easily into the narrative; in fact, if we
were only half-listening, the song would sound like one
of the typical folk ballads found in the beginning of this
book. There is also the easy "country and western" style
of Dylan's music and speech. But the most important
liberating element in the song is the magic of myth.

We do not refer to myth in its various fossilized forms, to
old tales one looks up in libraries. We mean myth as it can
be experienced here and now. Confronting a mythic story
or situation today, we find in it a pattern or image that
speaks to us not as individuals, but as members of a tribe.
We say "tribe" rather than "society" or "community"
because "tribe" connotes primitive connections between
men that sophisticated social organization suppresses or
obscures, and it is always within such relationships that
myth communicates. These mythic patterns and images
say nothing that can be confirmed by reason, for reason
is civilized language. Myths convey rather the "feel" of
how we are living, loving, praying, and dying, projecting
in sensible form the modes of our existence.

During this century, psychologists, anthropologists,
philosophers, and critics have given increasing attention
to the question of myth, and it is impossible, of course,
to summarize all these investigations within the space at
our disposal. The subject, however, is so important, both
for an understanding of Dylan's songs and of poetry in
general, that here we shall try to describe at least the
function of myth, though in necessarily simplified terms.

The basic situation from which myths originate is reflected
in the plot of Dylan's ballad. Living alone and without
commitment, Frankie Lee feels "mean" and dissatisfied.

Judas Priest, his "friend," is therefore able to tempt him with a vision of a place where Frankie can find a connection with God and man. The vision, however, proves false, and Frankie is destroyed rather than transformed. This story embodies a fundamental paradox of human existence. Like all living things, man seeks life, but life for man is consciousness. The more aware he is of himself and his environment, the more he lives—and *knows* he lives. This need for awareness can even be stronger than his fear of physical pain. We climb mountains, play at sports, take chances, and subject ourselves to the disciplines of a thousand games—craftsmanship, learning, art, religion, war, and so on—all for the sake of intensifying and expanding the light in our brains. But consciousness grows along two conflicting lines. On the one hand, it requires a strengthening of one's unique powers and sensibilities, or what might be loosely called one's self or "ego". On the other hand, it calls upon him to multiply his thoughts and feelings by absorbing those of his fellow men. These two requirements can lead to profound inner conflict. To live for and in others entails the destruction of the defensive, inward pointing ego, and yet that ego is the core of consciousness; not to be part of the group consciousness, however, is also to court mental death since awareness that is not social is not human. Considering Dylan's song in terms of this universal irony, we see that Frankie Lee's tragedy results not merely from the evil influence of a false religion, but from the conflicting demands of consciousness itself. The preacher reads them correctly when he tells us to find ourselves by losing ourselves, but Frankie's case shows how difficult that can be.

We turn next to the ways that myth enters into this tension between ego-centered and social, or "self-transcending," consciousness. But first we must see how ritual and art function in that connection. According to Carl Jung, Maude Bodkin, and other philosophers and psychologists, man works out the tensions of the permanent conflicts in his inner life by means of ritual and, later, of ritual turned into art. Participating in ritual or contemplating art, man asserts his ego by identifying with such substitutes as animals, heroes, priests, and kings in whom the power of the gods has become manifest, and yet also experiences the loss of ego in group consciousness through imaginatively sharing in the suffering and sacrifice of these ego substitutes. Presumably this is what accounts for the universal, enduring appeal of tragedy; of fertility and winter solstice rites in which the death of a god or a god representative is necessary for life to be reborn in the land; and of initiation ceremonies in which the childish ego is symbolically killed through trial and ordeal so that the young boy can assume the spirit of a warrior.

The specific content of these rituals and the drama, songs, dances, and stories which grow out of them is determined by whatever aspect of life the consciousness of a given tribe clusters around. Some life issues enter the rituals of all tribes and nations; notably, the conflict between fathers and sons and the universal fear of death. Others, such as those posed by the Christian religion, are limited to a particular civilization. Still others may be localized within a definite age of a civilization, for example, the issues of alienation and mechanization now dominating the Western world. Always, however, the form of the rituals is set by the internal contradictions of consciousness, the struggle of man to be both himself and a part of a greater Self experienced variously as clan, team, corporation, race, nation, God, and so on. Furthermore, it is always by means of *magic* that these rituals work out the contradictions of consciousness and the sub-conflicts that supply the content of those contradictions. What happens to us in them is akin to what happens in dreams. Ultimately, it is all inexplicable; but those to whom it happens may find it more convincing than logic, for the latter touches only the frailest surfaces of our minds, whereas the magic of ritual and art reaches the deepest layers of experience.

Given this necessarily grossly simplified picture of what drives men into ritual and art—or at least some ritual and art—we might now describe "myth" as a theme, story, or situation which is essential in a ritual working through an aspect of the self-contradictory career of consciousness. Living myths—the kind we are concerned about in *The Balled of Frankie Lee and Judas Priest*—can include both the old and new.

Old and still effective myths evoked in Dylan's song include the basic story of the god-possessed hero sacrificed by the priest and the re-birth of the hero in a child. They also include the Christian stories of the sinner in quest of salvation; Judas; the temptation of Christ in the wilderness; the agony of the pilgrim; and the ageless legend of the devil who masquerades as an angel. Then there is the old folk-song plot of the man who is betrayed by his best friend. All these ancient themes echoed in Dylan's ballad carry deep and wide-ranging associations for the tribal mind within us, for in them our tribe has objectivized recurrent experiences too profound to be expressed in rational terms.

But old myths are not enough to engage us fully. Today the modes of our relations to self and others are unique in history. We no longer can identify our egos with great heroes and kings in full seriousness (though perhaps we would still like to). We make such identifications only in fun; Batman and James Bond indicate just how absurd we think the superman really is. Furthermore, the manner in which we receive the thoughts and feelings of our tribe has profoundly changed. Now they come to us via a bombardment of disconnected messages and images, typified by the TV news report interlacing film clips of war and plane wrecks with ads for deodorants and dog food.

Acutely aware of what these differences mean for the "feel" of modern living, Dylan adjusts the old myths in his song to a relatively new one, that of the anti-hero, the little guy to whom everything happens and with whom we immediately identify. It is not, then, through the suffering and death of a great man that we are reborn, but through that of Frankie Lee, our helpless common denominator. Dylan also adjusts the presentation of his myths to reflect the new manner of communication between self and tribe, letting the myths filter through to us in random, incomplete, broken forms which we may or may not be able to put together—an analog of how we relate to the confluence of real life.

It is in this fragmented manner of presenting his myths that Dylan's surrealism comes into play. As indicated in our discussion of Robin Williamson, surrealism is basically radical juxtaposition of elements which defy rational con-nection. These elements can be images, as in Dylan's *Desolation Row,* or propositions, as in *Song of the Broken Giraffe,* a poem in the following section written by Bob Kaufman. In *The Ballad of Frankie Lee and Judas Priest,* the irrationally juxtaposed elements are mainly incidents.

Admittedly, they *almost* connect rationally, but on reflection, this false appearance only emphasizes their basic disconnection in the realm of ordinary sense and forces us to feel elsewhere for the links between them. But unlike many surrealist poems, Dylan's ballad seems to make that "elsewhere" readily available to us. Because of the contexts of the myths that he has made relevant, the realm of the plot emerges as something like the world of a nightmare we have not only dreamed but also somehow really lived, and as one incident follows another, we find ourselves saying, "Yes, that's how it goes."

The Ballad of Frankie Lee and Judas Priest

Words and Music by Bob Dylan
John Wesley Harding, Columbia CS 9604

Well, Frankie Lee and Judas Priest
They were the best of friends.
So when Frankie Lee needed money one day
Judas quickly pulled out a roll of tens;
And placed them on the footstool
Just above the cloudy plain
Saying "Take your pick, Frankie boy,
My loss will be your gain."

Well, Frankie Lee he sat right down
And put his fingers to his chin.
With the cold eyes of Judas on him
His head began to spin.
"Could you please not stare at me like that?" he said,
"It's just my foolish pride,
But sometimes a man must be alone
And this is no place to hide!"

Well Judas he just winked and said,
"All right, I'll leave you here.
But you better hurry up and choose which of those bills you want
Before they all disappear."
"I'm going to start picking right now.
Just tell me where you'll be."
Judas pointed down the road and said, "Eternity."

"Eternity?" said Frankie Lee
With a voice as cold as ice.
"That's right," said Judas, "Eternity,
Though you might call it paradise."
"I don't call it anything,"
Said Frankie Lee with a smile.
"All right," said Judas Priest,
"I'll see you after awhile."

Well, Frankie Lee, he sat back down
Feeling low and mean,
When just then a passing stranger
Burst upon the scene;
Saying "Are you Frankie Lee the gambler
Whose father is deceased?
If you are, there's a fellow calling you
        down the road,
And he says his name is Priest."

"Oh yes, he is my friend,"
Said Frankie Lee in fright.
"I do recall him very well
In fact he just left my sight."
"Yes, that's the one," said the stranger
As quiet as a mouse,
"All my message is, He's down the road
Stranded in a house."

Well, Frankie Lee, he panicked.
He dropped everything and ran;
Until he came unto the spot
Where Judas Priest did stand.
"What kind of house is this," he said
"Where I have come to roam?"
"It's not a house," said Judas Priest,
"It's not a house, it's a home."

Well, Frankie Lee he trembled,
He soon lost all control
Over everything which he had made
While the mission bell did toll,
He just stood there staring at the big house
As bright as any sun,
With four and twenty windows
And a woman's face in every one.

Well, up the stairs ran Frankie Lee
With a soulful bounding leap,
And foaming at the mouth
He began to make his midnight creep.
For sixteen nights and days he raved
But on the seventeenth he burst
Into the arms of Judas Priest
Which is where he died of thirst.

No one tried to say a thing
When they carried him out in jest.
Except of course the little
        neighbour boy
Who carried him to rest,
And he just walked along alone
With his guilt so well concealed,
And muttered underneath his breath,
"Nothing is revealed."

Well, the moral of this story,
The moral of this song,
Is simply that one should never be
Where one does not belong.
So when you see your neighbour
        carrying something
Help him with his load,
And don't go mistaking paradise
For that home across the road.

Sir Gawaine and the Green Knight
Yvor Winters

Reptilian green the wrinkled throat,
Green as a bough of yew the beard;
He bent his head, and so I smote;
Then for a thought my vision cleared.

The head dropped clean; he rose and walked;
He fixed his fingers in the hair;
The head was unabashed and talked;
I understood what I must dare.

His flesh, cut down, arose and grew.
He bade me wait the season's round,
And then, when he had strength anew,
To meet him on his native ground.

The year declined; and in his keep
I passed in joy a thriving yule;
And whether waking or in sleep,
I lived in riot like a fool.

He beat the woods to bring me meat.
His lady, like a forest vine,
Grew in my arms; the growth was sweet;
And yet what thoughtless force was mine!

By practice and conviction formed,
With ancient stubbornness ingrained,
Although her body clung and swarmed,
My own identity remained.

Her beauty, lithe, unholy, pure,
Took shapes that I had never known;
And had I once been insecure,
Had grafted laurel in my bone.

And then, since I had kept the trust,
Had loved the lady, yet was true,
The knight withheld his giant thrust
And let me go with what I knew.

I left the green bark and the shade,
Where growth was rapid, thick, and still;
I found a road that men had made
And rested on a drying hill.

The Little Vagabond
William Blake

Dear Mother, dear Mother, the Church is cold.
But the Ale-house is healthy & pleasant & warm;
Besides I can tell where I am use'd well,
Such usage in heaven will never do well.

But if at the Church they would give us some Ale,
And a pleasant fire, our souls to regale;
We'd sing and we'd pray, all the live-long day;
Nor ever once wish from the Church to stray,

Then the Parson might preach & drink & sing.
And we'd be as happy as birds in the spring:
And modest dame Lurch, who is always at Church,
Wou'ld not have bandy children nor fasting nor birch.

And God like a father rejoicing to see,
His children as pleasant and happy as he:
Would have no more quarrel with the Devil or the Barrel
But kiss him & give him both drink and apparel.

Carrion Comfort
Gerard Manley Hopkins

Not, I'll not, carrion comfort, Despair, not feast on thee;
Not untwist—slack they may be—these last strands of man
In me or, most weary, cry *I can no more.* I can;
Can something, hope, wish day come, not choose not to be.
But ah, but O thou terrible, why wouldst thou rude on me
Thy wring-world right foot rock? lay a lionlimb against me? scan
With darksome devouring eyes my bruisèd bones? and fan,
O in turns of tempest, me heaped there;
        me frantic to avoid thee and flee?
    Why? That my chaff might fly; my grain lie, sheer and clear.
Nay in all that toil, that coil, since (seems) I kissed the rod,
Hand rather, my heart lo! lapped strength,
        stole joy, would laugh, chéer.
Cheer whom though? the hero whose heaven-handling
        flung me, foot trod
Me? or me that fought him? O which one? is it each one?
        That night, that year
Of now done darkness I wretch lay wrestling
        with (my God!) my God.

Song of the Broken Giraffe

Bob Kaufman

I have heard the song of the broken giraffe, and sung it . . . .
The frozen sun has browned me to a rumor and slanted my navel.
I have consorted with vulgar crocodiles on banks of lewd rivers.
Yes, it is true, God has become mad, from centuries of frustration.
When I think of all the girls I never made love to, I am shocked.
Every time they elect me President, I hide in the bathroom.
When you come, bring me a tourniquet for our wounded moon.
In an emergency, I can rearrange your beautiful wreckage
With broken giraffe demolitions and lovely colorless explosions.
Come, you sexy Ferris wheel, ignore my illustrated bathing suit.
Don't laugh at my ignorance, I may be a great bullfighter, olé!
I wanted to compose a great mass, but I couldn't kneel properly.
Yes, they did tempt me with airplanes, but I wouldn't bite, no sir-ee.
Unable to avoid hospitals, I still refused to become a doctor.
They continued to throw reason, but I failed in the clutch again.
It's true, I no longer use my family as a frame of reference.
The clothing they gave me was smart but no good for train wrecks.
I continued to love despite all the traffic-light difficulties.
In most cases, a sane hermit will beat a good big man.
We waited in vain for the forest fire, but the bus was late.
All night we baked the government into a big mud pie.
Not one century passed without Shakespeare calling us dirty names.
With all those syllables, we couldn't write a cheerful death notice.
The man said we could have a birthday party if we surrendered.
Their soldiers refused to wear evening gowns on guard duty.
Those men in the basement are former breakfast-food salesmen.
We had a choice of fantasies, but naturally we were greedy.
If they leave me alone, I will become a fallen-leaf tycoon.
Maybe Peter Rabbit will forgive us our trespasses; one never knows.
At the moment of truth we were dancing a minuet and missed out.
After the nuns went home, the Pope threw a big masquerade ball.
When the hemlock turned rancid, I returned the cup at once, yes sir-ee.
Hurry, the barometer's falling; bring a storm before it's too late.
We shall reserve evenings for murder or television, whichever is convenient.
Yes, beyond a shadow of a doubt, Rumpelstiltskin was emotionally disturbed.

The Lay of the Battle of Tombland
Dunstan Thompson

"Whatever you want is yours,"
  Said the Man with the Lopside Head;
"Girls, diamonds, and motor cars,
  If you'll love me, love me in bed."

So he prayed, and the sirens sang
  Their wrongs, O sang to me
Lost in the blackout, "You're young
  But wait till you're old as we."

I stayed where I was, afraid
  To leave the Club Foot Man;
"Behind the mirror," he said, "we'll hide.
  The dead have a death-ray plan."

"Welcome! Welcome!" the searchlights wrote.
  "The End of the World is here."
They spelt their names and then went out,
  And the poor lay everywhere.

What could I cry but "Bombs Away,"
  When the Man who was Hunchback spoke.
"O live through this, and be my boy,"
  He laughed, and his true voice broke.

"God, be nimble," the dicers begged,
  "Christ, be quick;" but they rolled too short,
Their fears embraced, and the whirlers bragged
  "In our heartbreak arms is sport."

The Harelip Man knelt down to drink
  Blood from the sewers, swore
"You'll kiss me yet, and you'll thank
  Me later, later, after the war."

Through air of flares the statues ran
  Shrouded in silk. "Be warned,"
They wirelessed, "for marble men
  Are the friends you never mourned."

O bathed in fire my mobster stood,
    The Man with the Artificial Eyes,
"Falling in love with love," he said,
    "Is falling in love with lies."

This piteous city gave up the ghost
    In the toll of all her towers;
Parachute princes held me fast,
    "Rest," they ordered, "the rest is ours."

Rubaiyat of Omar Khayyam

Edward FitzGerald
(LXIII-LXIX)

O threats of Hell and Hopes of Paradise!
One thing at least is certain,—*This* Life flies;
    One thing is certain and the rest is Lies;
The Flower that once has blown for ever dies.

Strange, is it not? that of the myriads who
Before us passed the door of Darkness through
    Not one returns to tell us of the Road
Which to discover we must travel too.

The Revelations of Devout and Learn'd
Who rose before us, and as Prophets burn'd,
    Are all but Stories, which, awoke from Sleep
They told their fellows, and to Sleep return'd.

I sent my Soul through the Invisible,
Some letter of that After-life to spell:
    And by and by my Soul return'd to me,
And answered "I Myself am Heav'n and Hell":

Heav'n but the Vision of fulfill'd Desire,
And Hell the Shadow from a Soul on fire,
    Cast on the Darkness into which Ourselves,
So late emerged from, shall so soon expire.

We are no other than a moving row
Of Magic Shadow-shapes that come and go
    Round with this Sun-illumined Lantern held
In Midnight by the Master of the Show;

But helpless Pieces of the Game He plays
Upon this Chequer-board of Nights and Days;
    Hither and thither moves, and checks, and slays,
And one by one back in the Closet lays.

Easter Eve
Muriel Rukeyser

Wary of time O it seizes the soul tonight
I wait for the great morning of the west
confessing with every breath mortality.
Moon of this wild sky struggles to stay whole
and on the water silvers the ships of war.
I go alone in the black-yellow light
all night waiting for day, while everywhere the sure
death of light, the leaf's sure return to the root
is repeated in million, death of all man to share.
Whatever world I know shines ritual death,
wide under this moon they stand gathering fire,
fighting with flame, stand fighting in their graves.
All shining with life as the leaf, as the wing shines,
the stone deep in the mountain, the drop in the green wave.
Lit by their energies, secretly, all things shine.
Nothing can black that glow of life; although
                each part go crumbling down
                itself shall rise up whole.

Now I say there are new meanings; now I name
death our black honor and feast of possibility
to celebrate casting of life on life. This earth-long day
between blood and resurrection where we wait
remembering sun, seed, fire; remembering
that fierce Judaean Innocent who risked
every immortal meaning on one life.
Given to our year as sun and spirit are,
as seed we are blessed only in needing freedom.
Now I say that the peace the spirit needs is peace,
not lack of war, but fierce continual flame.
For all men: effort is freedom, effort's peace,
it fights. And along these truths the soul goes home,
                flies in its blazing to a place
                more safe and round than Paradise.

Night of the soul, our dreams in the arms of dreams
dissolving into eyes that look upon us.
Dreams the sources of action, the meeting and the end,
a resting-place among the flight of things.
And love which contains all human spirit, all wish,
the eyes and hands, sex, mouth, hair, the whole woman—
fierce peace I say at last, and the sense of the world.
In the time of conviction of mortality
whatever survive, I remember what I am.—
The nets of this night are on fire with sun and moon
pouring both lights into the open tomb.
Whatever arise, it comes in the shape of peace,
fierce peace which is love, in which moves all the stars,
and the breathing of universe, filling, falling away,
and death on earth cast into the human dream.
　　　　　What fire survive forever
　　　　　myself is for my time.

13

Buffy Sainte-Marie

In discussing the songs of Joni Mitchell, we said that their
charm is primarily due to the delicate balance she
maintains between involvement and detachment. Buffy
Sainte-Marie's songs also express an inner tension, but
the result is certainly not delicacy. On the contrary, what
comes through are emotions that strike like a force of
nature, and the tension we sense proceeds from Buffy's
struggle to keep them in rein.

A member of the Cree Indian tribe, Buffy Sainte-Marie,
like Joni Mitchell, was born in Saskatchewan. Also like
Joni, Buffy is now in the front rank of singer-composers
in North America. Her lyrics and music, however, are not
the principal source of her fame. In her songs, words
and music are a kind of membrane through which the
love, anger, grief, and indignation in her voice vibrate
with incredible intensity.

As her lyrics and music are intimately fused with the
energy and passion of her singing, we shall let her
recordings reveal the latent power of her words and forego
further comment. Let it simply be noted that there is sound
historical evidence to support the specific charges she
makes in the final song reprinted in this section,
My Country 'Tis of Thy People You're Dying, a protest
against North America's treatment of the once proud and
peaceful Indian nations.

The Universal Soldier

Words and Music by Buffy Sainte-Marie
It's My Way! Vanguard VSD 79142

He's five foot two and he's six feet four,
  he fights with missiles and with spears,
He's all of thirty-one and he's only seventeen,
  he's been a soldier for a thousand years.

He's a Catholic, a Hindu, an Atheist, a Jain,
  a Buddhist and a Baptist and a Jew,
And he knows he shouldn't kill and he knows he always will
  kill you for me, my friend, and me for you;

And he's fighting for Canada, he's fighting for France,
  he's fighting for the U.S.A.,
And he's fighting for the Russians and he's fighting for Japan,
  and he thinks we'll put an end to war that way.

And he's fighting for democracy, he's fighting for the Reds,
  he says it's for the peace of all,
He's the one who must decide who's to live and who's to die,
  and he never sees the writing on the wall.

But without him how would Hitler have condemned him at Dachau,
  without him Caesar would have stood alone.
He's the one who gives his body as a weapon of the war,
  and without him all this killing can't go on.

He's the Universal Soldier and he really is to blame,
  his orders come from far away no more,
They come from him and you and me, and, brothers can't you see,
  This is not the way we put an end to war.

i sing of Olaf

E. E. Cummings

i sing of Olaf glad and big
whose warmest heart recoiled at war:
a conscientious object-or

his well-belovéd colonel (trig
westpointer most succinctly bred)
took erring Olaf soon in hand;
but—though an host of overjoyed
noncoms (first knocking on the head
him) do through icy waters roll
that helplessness which others stroke
with brushes recently employed
anent this muddy toiletbowl,
while kindred intellects evoke
allegiance per blunt instruments—
Olaf (being to all intents
a corpse and wanting any rag
upon what God unto him gave)
responds,without getting annoyed
"I will not kiss your f.ing flag"

straightway the silver bird looked grave
(departing hurriedly to shave)

but—though all kinds of officers
(a yearning nation's blueeyed pride)
their passive prey did kick and curse
until for wear their clarion
voices and boots were much the worse,
and egged the firstclassprivates on
his rectum wickedly to tease
by means of skilfully applied
bayonets roasted hot with heat—
Olaf (upon what were once knees)
does almost ceaselessly repeat
"there is some s. I will not eat"

our president,being of which
assertions duly notified
threw the yellowsonofabitch
into a dungeon, where he died

Christ (of His mercy infinite)
i pray to see;and Olaf,too

preponderatingly because
unless statistics lie he was
more brave than me: more blond than you.

The Man He Killed

Thomas Hardy

"Had he and I but met
By some old ancient inn,
We should have sat us down to wet
Right many a nipperkin!

"But ranged as infantry,
And staring face to face,
I shot at him as he at me,
And killed him in his place.

"I shot him dead because–
Because he was my foe,
Just so: my foe of course he was;
That's clear enough; although

"He thought he'd 'list, perhaps,
Off-hand-like–just as I–
Was out of work–had sold his traps–
No other reason why.

"Yes, quaint and curious war is!
You shoot a fellow down
You'd treat, if met where any bar is,
Or help to half-a-crown."

1887

A. E. Housman

From Clee to heaven the beacon burns,
The shires have seen it plain,
From north and south the sign returns
And beacons burn again.

Look left, look right, the hills are bright,
The dales are light between,
Because 'tis fifty years tonight
That God has saved the Queen.

Now, when the flame they watch not towers
Above the soil they trod,
Lads, we'll remember friends of ours
Who shared the work with God.

To skies that knit their heartstrings right,
To fields that bred them brave,
The saviours come not home tonight:
Themselves they could not save.

It dawns in Asia, tombstones show
And Shropshire names are read;
And the Nile spills his overflow
Beside the Severn's dead.

We pledge in peace by farm and town
The Queen they served in war,
And fire the beacons up and down
The land they perished for.

"God save the Queen" we living sing,
From height to height 'tis heard;
And with the rest your voices ring,
Lads of the Fifty-third.

Oh, God will save her, fear you not:
Be you the men you've been,
Get you the sons your fathers got,
And God will save the Queen.

Confession

Morton Marcus

How do I say
that I'm a murderer?

I drag my shadow
as if it were a sack
full of discarded bodies.

My count is indefinite
but probably includes
the 8 mothers
who run through the caves
of my colon
with burning hair;

the baby
shaped like a scream;
the two girls
with hands and wombs
of flaming water;
and, on my spinal road,
the boy who crawls
farther and farther
from his legs.

I Have a Rendezvous with Death

Alan Seeger

I have a rendezvous with Death
At some disputed barricade,
When Spring comes back with rustling shade
And apple-blossoms fill the air—
I have a rendezvous with Death
When Spring brings back blue days and fair.
It may be he shall take my hand
And lead me into his dark land
And close my eyes and quench my breath—
It may be I shall pass him still.
I have a rendezvous with Death
On some scarred slope of battered hill,
When Spring comes round again this year
And the first meadow-flowers appear.

God knows 'twere better to be deep
Pillowed in silk and scented down,
Where love throbs out in blissful sleep,
Pulse nigh to pulse, and breath to breath,
Where hushed awakenings are dear . . .
But I've a rendezvous with Death
At midnight in some flaming town;
When Spring trips north again this year,
And I to my pledged word am true,
I shall not fail that rendezvous.

The Soldier
Rupert Brooke

If I should die, think only this for me:
    That there's some corner of a foreign field
That is for ever England. There shall be
    In that rich earth a richer dust concealed;
A dust whom England bore, shaped, made aware,
    Gave, once, her flowers to love, her ways to roam,
A body of England's, breathing English air,
    Washed by the rivers, blest by suns of home.

And think, this heart, all evil shed away,
    A pulse in the eternal mind, no less
    Gives somewhere back the thoughts by England given;
Her sights and sounds; dreams happy as her day;
    And laughter, learnt of friends; and gentleness,
        In hearts at peace, under an English heaven.

Anthem for Doomed Youth
Wilfred Owen

What passing-bells for these who die as cattle?
Only the monstrous anger of the guns.
Only the stuttering rifles' rapid rattle
Can patter out their hasty orisons.
No mockeries for them; no prayers nor bells,
Nor any voice of mourning save the choirs,–
The shrill, demented choirs of wailing shells;
And bugles calling for them from sad shires.

What candles may be held to speed them all?
Not in the hands of boys, but in their eyes
Shall shine the holy glimmers of good-byes.
The pallor of girls' brows shall be their pall;
Their flowers the tenderness of patient minds,
And each slow dusk a drawing-down of blinds.

Cain in Vietnam
David Bare

When you have tasted these things and know
the mud filled land fouled of flesh, the hand
will move against the heart, and you will drink
blood, and remember the earth
that passes through the worm.

And you will go to a city with four gates
surrounded by a ditch, and beyond the ditch
the walls of the city made high with stone,
and the four gates
strong with doors of brass.

These will be closed against you,
for though the beast rises from the sea
nothing will keep you but the sound of blood
rushing in your ears.

My Country 'Tis of Thy People You're Dying

Words and Music by Buffy Sainte-Marie
Buffy Sainte-Marie, *Little Wheel Spin & Spin*,
Vanguard VSD 79211

Now that your big eyes have finally opened
Now that you're wondering how must they feel
Meaning them that you've chased across America's movie screens
Now that you're wondering how can it be real
That the ones you call colorful, noble and proud
In your school propaganda
They starve in their splendor
You've asked for my comment, I simply will render

My country 'tis of thy people you're dying.

Now that the long houses breed superstition
You force us to send our toddlers away
To your schools where they're taught to despise their traditions
Forbid them their languages, then further say
That American history really began
When Columbus set sail out of Europe and stress
That the nation of leeches that conquered this land
Are the biggest and bravest, and boldest and best
And yet where in your history books is the tale
Of the genocide basic to this country's birth
Of the preachers that lied, how the Bill of Rights failed
How a nation of patriots returned to the earth
And where will it tell of the Liberty Bell
As it rang with a thud o'er the tinsel of mud
And of brave Uncle Sam in Alaska this year

My country 'tis of thy people you're dying.

Hear how the bargain was made for the West
With her shivering children in zero degrees
Blankets for your land so the treaties attest
Oh well, blankets for land is a bargain indeed
And the blankets were those Uncle Sam had collected
From smallpox disease dying soldiers that day
And the tribes were wiped out and the history books censored
A hundred years of your statesmen have felt it better this way
Yet a few of the conquered have somehow survived
Their blood runs redder though genes have been paled
From the Grand Canyon's caverns to the Craven Red Hills
The wounded, the losers, the rod sings their tale
From Los Angeles county to upstate New York
The white nation fattens while others grow lean
Oh, the tricked and evicted, they know what I mean

My country 'tis of thy people you're dying.

The past it just crumbled, the future just threatens
Our lifeblood shut up in your chemical tanks
And now here you come, bill of sale in your hand
And surprise in eyes that we're lacking in thanks
For the blessings of civilization you brought us
The lessons you've taught us, the ruin you've wrought us
Oh, see what our trust in America's brought us

My country 'tis of thy people you're dying.

Now that the pride of the sires receive charity
Now that we're harmless and safe behind laws
Now that my life's to be known as your heritage
Now that even the graves have been robbed
Now that our own chosen way is a novelty
Hands on our hearts, we salute you your victory
Choke on your blue, white and scarlet hypocrisy
Pitying the blindness that you've never seen
That the eagles of war whose wings lent you glory
They were never no more than carrion crows
Push the wrens from their nest, stow their eggs, change their story
The mockingbird sings it, it's all that she knows
Oh, what can I do, say a powerless few
With a lump in your throat and a tear in your eye,
Can't you see that our poverty's profiting you?

My country 'tis of thy people you're dying.

Death of the American Indian's God

Gregory Corso

The Mandan village is covered with snow
The blanketed chiefs on parfleches blow
Women in tufts of weasel press tapioca
And the lacrosse game is almost over–
Fling wompsikkucks at the Evening Star
The Mighty One Tirawa Atius is lain
    on the bright travois

He in His own raced hills and valleys
    wore skins birds and calumets
He in His own the laughing Koyemshi
    dogclowned all our sunsets
Give proper ceremony O Pawnee
The last caribou has been arrowed
    the last trout speared
Beetle bells and medicine yells
Everyone is dressed in crow

    They were the redmen
    feathers-in-their-head men
    now
    down among the dead men
    how

The Forsaken
Duncan Campbell Scott

I
Once in the winter
Out on a lake
In the heart of the north-land,
Far from the Fort
And far from the hunters,
A Chippewa woman
With her sick baby,
Crouched in the last hours
Of a great storm.
Frozen and hungry,
She fished through the ice
With a line of the twisted
Bark of the cedar,
And a rabbit-bone hook
Polished and barbed;
Fished with the bare hook
All through the wild day,
Fished and caught nothing;
While the young chieftain
Tugged at her breasts,
Or slept in the lacings
Of the warm *tikanagan*.
All the lake-surface
Streamed with the hissing
Of millions of iceflakes
Hurled by the wind;
Behind her the round
Of a lonely island
Roared like a fire
With the voice of the storm
In the deeps of the cedars.

Valiant, unshaken,
She took of her own flesh,
Baited the fish-hook,
Drew in a grey-trout,
Drew in his fellows,
Heaped them beside her,
Dead in the snow.
Valiant, unshaken,
She faced the long distance,
Wolf-haunted and lonely,
Sure of her goal
And the life of her dear one:
Tramped for two days,
On the third in the morning,
Saw the strong bulk
Of the Fort by the river,
Saw the wood-smoke
Hang soft in the spruces,
Heard the keen yelp
Of the ravenous huskies
Fighting for whitefish:
Then she had rest.

II

Years and years after,
When she was old and withered,
When her son was an old man
And his children filled with vigour,
They came in their northern tour on the verge of winter,
To an island in a lonely lake.
There one night they camped, and on the morrow
Gathered their kettles and birth-bark,
Their rabbit-skin robes and their mink-traps,
Launched their canoes and slunk away through the islands,
Left her alone forever,
Without a word of farewell,
Because she was old and useless,
Like a paddle broken and warped,
Or a pole that was splintered.
Then, without a sigh,
Valiant, unshaken,
She smoothed her dark locks under her kerchief,
Composed her shawl in state,
Then folded her hands ridged with sinews and corded with veins,
Folded them across her breasts spent with the
      nourishing of children,
Gazed at the sky past the tops of the cedars,
Saw two spangled nights arise out of the twilight,
Saw two days go by filled with the tranquil sunshine,
Saw, without pain, or dread, or even a moment of longing:
Then on the third great night there came thronging
      and thronging
Millions of snowflakes out of a windless cloud;
They covered her close with a beautiful crystal shroud,
Covered her deep and silent.
But in the frost of the dawn,
Up from the life below,
Rose a column of breath
Through a tiny cleft in the snow,
Fragile, delicately drawn,
Wavering with its own weakness,
In the wilderness a sign of the spirit,
Persisting still in the sight of the sun
Till day was done.
Then all light was gathered up by the hand of God
      and hid in His breast,
Then there was born a silence deeper than silence,
Then she had rest.

About the Poets

Prepared especially for
secondary school students
by Kenneth J. Weber

Matthew Arnold (1822-1888)
was a scholar, essayist, critic,
and poet. His poetry is often
subjected to as much abuse as
praise, ranging as it does from
the pedantic to the subtly beau-
tiful and haunting. Throughout
his life he was plagued with
spiritual dilemmas, especially
in his attempt to find "real faith"
through reason. His poetry
reflects a Classical leaning,
probably because of his belief
in the pursuit of intellectual
excellence. Nevertheless,
some of Arnold's best work is
in the style generally associated
with the Romantics.

Wystan Hugh Auden (b. 1907)
is an English-born, American
poet and scholar who toyed
with Marxism in the 1930's, but
has become less politically
radical since. His poetry is
intellectual and marked by
sharp and witty observations
of our society.

David Bare (b. 1944)
is now studying for an M.A. in
English at the University of
Toronto, where he has won
three Epstein and one Frederick
Davidson prizes in poetry.

William Blake (1757-1827),
a mystic whose poetry is filled
with images of intense feeling,
was appalled by the creeping
materialism of his age and
sought a hopeful alternative in
visionary religion. Generally
considered a pre-Romantic or
early Romantic, he is in many
ways like early twentieth-century
poets in style and content.

Edwin Brock (b. 1917)
has been a policeman by voca-
tion and a poet by avocation.
This unusual combination may
account for the very forthright
style of his poetry. One critic,
in praising Brock's work, has
said that the ideas in his poems
often appear to be "hammered"
into verse. Brock himself has
said that "when there has been
significance in experience, it
may be communicated by an
extreme honesty of description."

Rupert Brooke (1887-1915)
was a graduate of Cambridge,
but is said to have developed a
deep love of his country during
his travels outside it. Many of
his most patriotic poems were
written during the beginning
of World War I.

**Elizabeth Barrett Browning
(1806-1861)**
is perhaps most popularly
known for her romantic elope-
ment with Robert Browning.
Although she had been a semi-
invalid in her father's home in
England, life in Italy, where she
lived with Browning, seemed to
improve her health. Much of her
literary reputation rests on letters
and love sonnets she wrote to
Browning during their courtship
and marriage.

Robert Browning (1812-1889)
wrote short lyrics, long poetic
dramas, and fascinating psy-
chological analyses; but his
greatest work is probably the
perfection of the dramatic
monologue form. In a vigorous
and elliptical style he cham-
pioned self-fulfillment, liberty,
and optimism. As he lived in
Italy for many years, the
Renaissance came to exert a
strong influence on his work.

John Bruce (b. 1922)
has published poetry in *Northern
Review, Canadian Forum,
Fiddlehead, Delta,* and *Canadian
Poetry.* He is now chairman of
the philosophy department at the
University of Guelph, Ontario.

**George Gordon, Lord Byron
(1788-1824)**
might be the one poet in English
literary history whose biography
is read as frequently as his
poetry. A wealthy and handsome
man, he stirred up such gossip
in England that he eventually
left for the Continent. Although

Byron once said of his own poetry that "No one has done more through negligence to corrupt the language," any flaws in his poetry are probably the result of overwhelming energy.

Thomas Campion (1567-1619), a contemporary of Shakespeare, was a musician as well as a poet. Much of his poetry was set to music which he composed. The effect is the delicate, sentimental tone of his poetry, and especially the metrical polish of the verse.

Thomas Carew (1595-1639) was one of the best of the courtly poets of the seventeenth century. His poems show exceptionally careful attention to form and construction. Short lyrics of tender beauty and delicate expression characterize his work.

Gregory Corso (b. 1930) is one of the most important poets of the "Beat Generation". He has travelled widely and his poetry usually reflects the environment in which he wrote at the time. Corso has said that poetry is the element that lights up the darkness of the world for him and enables him to perceive what others cannot see.

Stephen Crane (1871-1900), an American, is known primarily as a novelist, and particularly for his novel *The Red Badge of Courage*. Throughout his brief career as a war correspondent and writer, he suffered from both ill health and malicious gossip. The style of his poetry is clipped and cryptic, more in the modern vein than in the Victorian.

E. E. Cummings (1894-1962) was an American who won early attention as a painter and draughtsman in Europe. What would otherwise be simple satire is given a special dimension in his poetry through the use of unusual syntax, typography, and word combinations.

John Davidson (1857-1909) was a Scottish playwright, novelist, and poet whose life was one of intense poverty and melancholy. Davidson's life and work belie the popular romantic notion of the artist starving himself for the sake of his art. He once wrote to a friend: "Nine-tenths of my time has been wasted trying to earn a livelihood." Critics have said his work is filled with insight, but often rough and uneven in style. Much of his creative work reflects the melancholy and frustration of his life.

C. Day-Lewis (b. 1904), a native of Ireland, achieved his fame in England. He is a long-time friend and associate of W. H. Auden, and their poems are frequently cited as effective expressions of social discontent.

Emily Dickinson (1830-1886) is perhaps the best known woman poet of America. Although she led a secluded, quiet life in New England, her poetry was ahead of its time in conception and technique. Much of her poetry is characterized by a delightful and unusual use of ordinary language. Her poetry, which seems so relevant today, remained generally unpublished during her lifetime.

John Donne (1573-1631) was an English poet of the Metaphysical school. His career ranged from what we now know as the civil service to the ministry. Donne's poetry presents a strange mixture of theology and human love, in a style that is distinguished by its use of grandiose metaphors.

Michael Drayton (1563-1631), a writer of apparently limitless energy, is credited with numerous volumes of poetry, as well as several plays, and other prose works. Although his work is somewhat uneven in quality, his verses are always highly polished.

Lawrence Ferlinghetti (b. 1919), an American poet, was instrumental in making the West Coast attractive as a haven for budding young writers. His poetry, always written in the contemporary idiom, expresses his deep concern with the barriers that contemporary society builds between people.

Edward FitzGerald (1809-1883) will be remembered for what is still regarded as the best translation of *The Rubaiyat of Omar Khayyam,* although the majority of his work was overshadowed by other "greats" of the Victorian era. FitzGerald used several translations of *The Rubaiyat* (in several languages) to create a work that captures better than any other the spirit of the Persian philosopher-poet.

Robert Frost (1874-1963) can be considered the dean of twentieth-century American poets. His poetry is distinguished by an apparently simple, rural outlook and is expressed in rhythmic speech suggestive of the "common" man. Yet, at the same time, he frequently touches on the most timeless themes of life in such a way that future American poets may live under his shadow for a long time to come.

St. Denys Garneau (1912-1943) was a prominent figure in French Canadian literature of the early twentieth century. Given to solitude and reflectiveness in his personal life, his work frequently touches on such subjects as death, loneliness, sadness, and silence.

Robert Graves (b. 1895) is one of the most eminent men of letters of the twentieth century. He has made significant contributions to the fields of Roman history, mythological

research, and literary criticism, in addition to his novels, translations, and his poetry.

Fulke Greville (1554-1628) was a friend and faithful follower of Sir Philip Sidney, whose influence on Greville's work was quite profound. Greville is credited with some drama and prose, as well as poetry. His talent in the latter field lies chiefly in the metrical polish of his verse.

Thomas Hardy (1840-1928) was a literary giant whose lifetime spanned many of the great social and political events that have affected the course of the twentieth century. Although he is generally associated with the Victorian period of literature, his work is not typical of that era. Hardy reveals in his poetry and his novels a deep awareness of the ironies of life and the weaknesses of humanity.

John Harney (b. 1931), a native of Quebec, has combined the careers of university teacher, politician, and poet. His poetry has appeared in *Poetry, Fiddlehead, Delta, Canadian Forum, Alphabet,* and the anthology of Canadian poetry, *Poetry '62.* He is presently provincial secretary of the New Democratic Party of Ontario.

Gerard Manley Hopkins (1844-1889) was an Oxford graduate who became a convert to Roman Catholicism and, ultimately, a Jesuit priest. His poetry was not published until after his death, primarily because the literary fashion of the time would probably not have accepted his "sprung" rhythms and unusual word order.

Alfred Edward Housman (1859-1936) was an English poet whose published writing is slight in quantity but not in quality. He described the art of writing poetry as a fever that cannot be endured for long periods of time; this may account for the fact that he published only two slim volumes during his lifetime. In his poetry there is a sense of inevitable doom, and although his verse forms are traditional and conventional, there is beauty in the imagery and a singing rise and fall to the rhythm.

James Langston Hughes (1902-1967)
was one of the most popular black American poets of this century. His style is distinguished by his ability to create an atmosphere of tenderness and quiet pathos. Yet, he can also create images that repel and frighten when dealing with the plight of American black people.

Ted Hughes (b. 1930),
an English poet, had won several writing awards by the age of 30. Marianne Moore said his work "is aglow with feeling, with conscience; sensibility is awake, embodied in appropriate diction."

Ben Jonson (1572-1637),
a contemporary of Shakespeare, is better known for his satirical drama than for his poetry. Although his dramas abound in the exuberant language of the street, his poems are models of civility and grace.

Bob Kaufman (b. 1931),
discovered by Lawrence Ferlinghetti, was first published by Ferlinghetti in two City Lights broadsides. His most recent volume is *Solitudes Crowded with Loneliness* (New Directions, 1965), a work that places him in the front ranks of American Negro poets.

John Keats (1795-1821)
wrote his own epitaph: "Here lies one whose name was writ in water." His poetry is melan-

choly and haunted with a sad beauty. His life was a succession of sorrows—he lost his brother to consumption; learned that he had it himself; and was rejected by his fiancée—all within a few short years. Although Keats was criticized severely in his first years as a poet, few other writers have left such a legacy of highly reputed works. Sensuous, passionate, concrete in detail and imagery, yet suggestive in emotion and atmosphere, his poetry is probably the most romantic of the Romantics.

Philip Larkin (b. 1922),
an English poet whose work is frequently concerned with the frustrations and feelings of ordinary people, is also a university librarian. Along with his other accomplishments, he is an expert on jazz, the influence of which can be seen in his poetry.

Irving Layton (b. 1912)
is a gifted Canadian poet whose celebration of the sensuous has always stirred up controversy. His craftsmanship is superb, and with it he manages to control what seems to be random imagery and form.

Amy Lowell (1874-1925),
a member of a prominent New England family, belonged to a group of writers who called themselves the Imagist Poets. Their object was to convey their thoughts and feelings in clear, precise images, shunning utterly anything mystical or vague. It is this concrete language and vivid imagery that marks Amy Lowell's poetry.

Louis MacNiece (b. 1907)
is a poet of satire and irony. He gained fame between the two world wars and is generally considered closely allied to W. H. Auden and C. Day-Lewis. Although lyrical verse is not his

forte, such occasional pieces as *Snow* show the breadth of his poetic ability.

Linda Marshall (b. 1941) teaches English at the University of Guelph and is preparing for a doctorate in medieval studies at the University of Toronto. She is co-editor of the Canadian literary periodical, *Grub.*

Andrew Marvell (1621-1678) was a poet of great wit and imagination, capable of building fluent rhythmic patterns, especially in his use of "conceits". His best poems are considered by most critics to be unsurpassable.

Edgar Lee Masters (1869-1950) was an American poet and novelist whose financial security was assured by his thriving law practice in the Midwest. Although much of his work goes unnoticed, his *Spoon River Anthology* is considered to be among the landmarks of twentieth-century American literature. In this work, Masters presents a series of epitaphs, spoken from the cemetery of the mythical town of Spoon River.

Paul Maurice (b. 1945) is a young Canadian poet, presently majoring in English at the University of Guelph in Ontario. His poems have appeared in *Canadian Forum* and *Mountain Poetry Newsletter.*

George Meredith (1828-1909) was an English poet of lower-class birth and aristocratic tastes. His unhappy marriage apparently was a stimulating force behind the composition of *Modern Love.* These poems are notable for their various styles, powerful uses of language, and many psychological insights.

Maria Nunez is from Almunecar, Grenada, Spain. She has published poetry in the Spanish journal, *The Seashell,* and Argentine poetry periodicals. Now a Canadian citizen, residing in Toronto, she is just beginning to write poems in English.

Wilfred Owen (1893-1918) is most famous for his strong, occasionally vicious anti-war poetry, which ran counter to the highly patriotic feeling predominant during World War I, as expressed by such poets as Rudyard Kipling. He gave the fighting man's point of view instead of the homefront patriot's. He was killed just a week before the armistice. Owen is very like modern lyricists both in the strength of his feelings and the elliptical quality of his style. He frequently uses assonance rather than rhyme.

Edgar Allan Poe (1809-1849), an American poet, essayist, novelist, and short story writer, is usually associated in a popular sense with the mysterious and the macabre. Although his personal life was an almost incredible series of misfortunes, Poe left some brilliant works, especially on the subjects of beauty, love, and death. He was essentially a lyric poet and made great use of sonorous words, frequent repetition, long lines, refrains, and splendid, melodious phrases.

Edwin John Pratt (1883-1964) was born in Newfoundland and reared in a manse. He was endowed with an awareness of nature and a feeling for his fellow man that combine to produce a humanist poetry. His style ranges from an almost breezy use of technical language to simple, natural speech.

Sir Walter Ralegh (c. 1552-1618), whose poetry was described by one of his contemporaries as "most lofty, insolent, and passionate," wrote with the analytical and satirical tone of the seventeenth century rather than in the Elizabethan spirit.

Tim Reynolds (b. 1936)
is a native of Mississippi and
supports himself largely by
writing. He is fluent in several
languages, a significant advan-
tage, given his penchant for
research into obscure subjects.
Not all of his poetry reflects the
bitterness evident in *A Hell
Of A Day,* although it is fre-
quently concerned with contem-
porary problems.

Christina Rossetti (1830-1894)
was a member of the pre-
Raphaelite group in England.
Her poetry is simple and spon-
taneous. Her religious devotion
is reflected in the symbolism
and allegory of her work.

Muriel Rukeyser (b. 1913)
is a prolific American poet
known for her keen sense of
observation. Her output includes
essays, biographies, and
children's books.

Penelope Schafer,
known professionally only as
"Penelope," was born in
Victoria, British Columbia, and
has lived in Halifax, Vancouver,
and Toronto. Her activities
include public relations work
for the Toronto *Telegram* and
Canadian Art; writing pop lyrics
and radio scripts for the Cana-
dian Broadcasting Corporation;
managing a rock band; writing
and acting in a feature film,
Zero, the Fool; and reading
poetry at the Mariposa Festival
and universities throughout
Ontario.

Alan Seeger (1888-1916)
was an English poet and an
uncle of Pete Seeger. Although
critics have generally rated him
as a minor poet, most of them
agree that *I Have a Rendezvous
With Death* assures Seeger a
place in the history of English
literature. Seeger died in the
trenches in World War I. He was
wounded in a charge across
"No-Man's Land" and was last
seen alive urging his comrades
to victory. His body was found
in a shell hole the next day.

**William Shakespeare
(1564-1616)**
composed poetry of such bril-
liance and vitality that even if
he had not produced a single
play he would still be renowned
today.

Karl Shapiro (b. 1913)
is an American poet, editor,
essayist, and university profes-
sor. He has a unique way of
using current, everyday lan-
guage to give poetic grace to
what on the surface appear to
be unpoetic subjects.

**Percy Bysshe Shelley
(1792-1822)**
is a classic example of the
Romantic and social rebel; even
Shelley's death by drowning
came about partially as an act
of defiance. Elaborate yet beau-
tiful imagery characterizes his
poetry, as he attempts to express
spiritual qualities. Shelley tries
to speak directly to the heart of
his reader, and the consequent
lack of precision occasionally
leads to obscurity. Nevertheless,
his poetry is a testament to the
spontaneity and imagination in
which he believed.

Raymond Souster (b. 1912)
is a Toronto banker and poet
who is known for his witty use of
everyday speech. His work fre-
quently takes the form of short
vignettes or lyrical portraits.

William Stafford (b. 1914)
is an American university pro-
fessor who is held in very high
regard for his literary criticism.

Allen Tate (b. 1899)
is an American poet who, like
William Stafford, is more widely
known for his criticism than his
poetry. His approach is usually
an intellectual one, as can be
seen from his diction.

**Alfred, Lord Tennyson
(1809-1892)**
was the poetic voice for Victorian
sentiment. His great skill was in

his use of imitative harmony and imagery. Unlike many other poets, he was probably more famous during his lifetime than after. As the mores of Victorian life fell into disrepute, Tennyson, their spokesman, fell with them.

Dylan Thomas (1914-1953) remains a legend, both for his poetry and his colorful personal life. Thomas' explosive and sensuous diction and his unusual juxtapositions create many levels of meaning. His poetry has a way of evoking in the reader a sense of private, yet commonly shared, experience.

Dunstan Thompson (b. 1918) was born in Connecticut, but now makes his home in England. His personal interests range from research in witchcraft to ecclesiastical literature. Although his recent published works are scant, he is still regarded as a writer of some prominence.

Thomas Traherne (c. 1636-1674) was an English writer of both prose and verse. His best poetry is that written from the point of view of the child.

Henry Vaughan (1622-1695) was an English poet who was literally unknown until the mid-nineteenth century. *The World* is among the religious poems that helped to establish his reputation.

Paul Vesey (b. 1917) is the professional name of Samuel W. Allen. An attorney and teacher of law, Vesey has won recognition in Europe as an important American Negro poet. Richard Wright first published his poems in the French journal, *Présence Africaine.* In Germany, Wolfgang Hoth Verlag published his work in *Elfenbein Zahne (Ivory Tusks)* in 1956.

Margaret Walker (b. 1915) is a native of Alabama and has taught English at Livingstone College, Salisbury, North Carolina, and West Virginia State College. Her first book of poetry, *For My People,* won the Yale University Younger Poets competition and was published in 1942.

Isaac Watts (1674-1748) was a clergyman whose creative works include *Divine Songs For Children,* and the famous hymn, *O' God Our Help In Ages Past.* He was one of the first writers of hymns and religious verse to break away from Biblical paraphrase into the broad imagery and imagination of a poet.

Walt Whitman (1819-1892), a robust, uninhibited poet, was in constant difficulty with his contemporaries. With his aggressive style, Whitman spoke as interpreter of life and prophet of America's greatness. His influence on subsequent American poets has been profound.

Yvor Winters (b. 1900) is an American poet best known for his scholarly criticisms of poetry. Much of his poetry and his critical work is based on the premise that art, in his words, is "an act of moral judgment".

William Wordsworth (1770-1850), co-author with Samuel Taylor Coleridge of the famous *Lyrical Ballads,* is often considered the father of the Romantic movement in poetry. Wordsworth's work has been both praised and damned. Although it is generally philosophical, it lacks the melody and grace of the other Romantic poets. He is at his best in his lyrical celebrations of nature.

Elinor Wylie (1885-1928) was an American poet equally well known for her novels. *I Hereby Swear That To Uphold Your House* is typical of the lyrical qualities of her verse.

Suggestions for Study

Prepared especially for secondary school students
by Kenneth J. Weber

Section 1: Folk Songs and Blues

Black Is the Color
(as sung by Joan Baez)

1. a) Explain how each of *Black Is the Color, Song of Solomon,* and *Shall I Compare Thee to a Summer's Day* (Sonnet 18), creates an impression of total, even worshipful, love.
   b) For each of the selections in (a), outline the form, the tone, and the basic type of imagery.
   c) To what degree is an expression of love affected by the form and manner in which it is presented?

2. To the modern ear, lines such as
   "his belly is as bright ivory overlaid with sapphires"
   (Song of Solomon)
   and
   "There is a garden in her face" (title and first line of the poem by Thomas Campion)
   border on the ridiculous, especially as statements of admiration. Yet few people react the same way to
   "The purest eyes and the bravest hands" *(Black Is the Color).*
   Why is this so?

3. Are any of the selections in this unit too exaggerated? Do you find this exaggeration embarrassing or offensive?

4. Read several of the love poems for a tape recording. Note carefully what attitude, voice pitch, and pace the reader adopts for each poem. Can you account for any changes in the reader's style?

Cherry Tree Carol
(as sung by Joan Baez)

5. A critic might argue that *Cherry Tree Carol* would have great *immediate* impact as a religious experience, but that Hopkins' *God's Grandeur* would have a more *lasting* effect. Do you agree?

6. Note carefully the techniques of the lyricist as outlined in the introduction to this section. How has Hopkins used almost all these lyrical techniques within the confining structure of a sonnet?

Johnny I Hardly Knew Yeh
(as sung by The Clancy Brothers)

7. Explain how each of the selections in this unit creates an ironic effect.

8. Can the horrors of war be effectively presented in the form of a song? Is the Clancy Brothers' version effective?

9. Reynolds' technique in *A Hell of a Day* is designed to shock the reader. Is he successful? Does the lyrical presentation of *Johnny I Hardly Knew Yeh* ease the shock? In your opinion, is poetry more powerful for the basic, serious subjects of life, whereas songs are more suitable for lighter and more suggestive topics?

Stackerlee
(as sung by Dave Van Ronk)

10. Compare with others your feelings about the principal characters in *Stackerlee* and *Jonne Armestrong.* Which of the two "heroes" is the more believable? Why do some people identify with Stackerlee, even though he is unreal?

Follow The Drinkin' Gourd

11. Explain how two so vastly different works as *Follow The Drinkin' Gourd* and *Song of Myself* could come from the same tradition— slavery. Does the great difference between the two explain why one was written as a poem and the other became a song?

12. What effect is achieved by the prayer-like structure of Margaret Walker's *For My People?*

John Henry
(as sung by Sonny Terry and Brownie McGhee)

13. For each selection in this unit, describe the attitude of the writer toward his subject. What evidence supports your opinion?

14. Explain the methods by which each writer outlines both situation and background.
    Woman Blue
    (as sung by Judy Roderick)
15. Which of *Woman Blue* and *I Hereby Swear That to Uphold Your House* is the more convincing profession of love?
16. Why is the "sense of wonder" increased in both poem and lyric by leaving things unsaid?
    Death Don't Have No Mercy
    (as sung by Rev. Gary Davis)
17. Discuss the appropriateness of the *form* each writer in this unit has used to talk about death.
18. Why is death such a popular subject in poetry and song?

Section 2: Pete Seeger

1. a) The poems and lyrics in this section share what the introduction calls a "living room" effect. Consider several of the selections and outline the various means by which this effect is achieved.
   b) For what reasons do some poems and lyrics have a more *involving* effect than others?
2. Explain why some of the poems in this section have more emotional appeal than others.
3. a) Why do Seeger's lyrics such as *My Father's Mansions,* and poems such as Blake's *I Give You the End of a Golden String* or Auden's *The Shield of Achilles* leave so much unsaid?
   b) Do the specific details in *Talking Union* and in Whitman's *Thou Mother with Thy Equal Brood* diminish the impact?
4. Why are symbolism and allegory such vital means of developing a close emotional association between the creator and his audience? Explain your answer by reference to several works in this section.
5. Whitman, Blake, and Seeger use the techniques of prayer in the poetry of this section. Point out the presence of these techniques in several of the selections, and assess their effectiveness.
6. On what bases could you compare *Talking Blues* and Shelley's *Song to the Men of England*?
7. How might you compare Blake's *The New Jerusalem* and Seeger's *Talking Union*?
8. a) Does Auden gain or lose in effect by intermingling what seems to be two poems in *The Shield of Achilles*?
   b) Would Seeger have diminished the impact of *The Big Muddy* if he had eliminated the last verse?
9. Which of *The Shield Of Achilles* or *The Big Muddy* is likely to have the greater influence on our feelings about war in years to come?
10. *Who Knows*
    Since Brass, nor Stone, nor Earth
    To His Coy Mistress
    Do any of the feelings or attitudes of optimism, pessimism, realism, or hedonism find expression in the poems listed above? If so, how are these feelings created?
11. The Introduction suggests that it might be unwise to consider Seeger's lyrics strictly as lyrics, his music as music. Bearing this in mind, try to discover differences between the lyrics from Section I and Seeger's work.
12. Using a tape recorder, have different students in the group prepare readings of the same poems. Analyze the differences in the readings, and try to evaluate how successfully each reader *involves* his listeners.

Section 3: Tim Buckley

1. *Note:* The following questions on Tim Buckley's *Goodbye and Hello* and its companion poems are designed to assist discussion of the five aspects of the lyrics outlined in the introduction to this section.
   a) world outlook
   What advice does Vaughan imply as he presents his vision of eternity in *The World*? What will be the motivating forces in the world that Shelley foresees in *The World's Great Age*? Show that Buckley in *Goodbye and Hello* holds views similar to those of Arnold, but that he differs in attitude. Do Vaughan and Buckley differ only in the solutions they suggest for the world's problems? To which of the four poets is Buckley most similar in attitude? Is Ferlinghetti's poem *I Am Waiting* a reminder to man to mend his

ways before it is too late, or is it simply a statement of pessimism, an acknowledgement of the fact that it is already too late?

b) perspective of the child
Precisely how did Traherne see the world when he was born? What suggestion is there in *Wonder* that disillusion was inevitable? Both these elements (wonder and disillusion) are present in *Goodbye and Hello,* but how do Buckley's children react to them? Does the narrative style of *The Game* suggest that the wonder of childhood doesn't last?

c) attitude toward the body
Describe how Buckley, and Whitman in *A Woman Waits for Me,* express an almost identical attitude toward sex, but in different ways. Would John Donne, if he were alive, condone Buckley's attitude toward the body?

d) attitude toward country
Both Buckley, and Wilfred Owen in *Dulce et Decorum Est,* reject intense patriotism, but their reasons differ; explain how this difference is revealed in the technique of each work. Show how Shakespeare achieves such power in John of Gaunt's death speech *This Royal Throne of Kings.* Does this speech, when compared with *Goodbye and Hello,* make the lyric less profound?

e) perspective of the puritan
How does Stafford's *One Home* convey a sense of self-righteousness? In what way does this poem explain much that *Goodbye and Hello* opposes? Does *The Lotos-Eaters* actually praise hedonism, or is there an element of criticism in the poem? What differences in outlook exist between Tennyson's poem and those sections of the lyric beginning "O the new children . . ."?

2. Most poetry involves a certain amount of mythology, or a body of known and widely accepted material, to which it can allude, thereby establishing in a brief stroke all the meaning that might be otherwise impossible to express.
a) Identify the source of most of the allusions in any three poems from this section and Buckley's lyric.
b) Do the source and the allusions in each case automatically limit the audience?

Section 4: Joni Mitchell
Marcie
1. a) A critic has said that Joni Mitchell's work is like a painting done in watercolors. Explain how the images, the choice of words, the atmosphere, and the narrative line in *Marcie* reflect the impression given by a watercolor painting.
b) On the other hand, Amy Lowell's *Patterns* might be likened to a sharply defined oil painting with striking colors. Explain how her poem fits this pattern.
c) Which poem evokes a greater feeling of pathos?
Michael from Mountains
2. Although both the lyric and the Wordsworth poem here present a picture of the beauty of childhood, *Michael from Mountains* seems to create a more authentic, more acceptable picture of what childhood is really like. Consider the reasons for this.
Nathan La Franeer
3. a) All three works presented here are critical of society, but does each suggest a different reason for society's degeneration?
b) "Every time I feel a certain way about something, I hear an argument for the other side. I'm just a hopeless middleman." (Joni Mitchell in an interview with Peter Goddard for the Toronto *Telegram,* 1969). Show how *Nathan La Franeer* is essentially a protest song, and yet not entirely a one-sided picture.
c) Compare Blake's *London* with *Nathan La Franeer* from the following points of view: i) strength of the images, ii) effect of the first-person delivery, iii) breadth of the vision.
Song to a Seagull
4. a) By contrasting this lyric with one of its companion poems that is more concrete, show how images, connotations of words, and the sentiments in *Song to a Seagull* create an atmosphere of fragility.
b) Would the melancholy of *Ode to a Nightingale* be heightened or lessened if it were put to music—any kind of music?
c) Note carefully the techniques by which Joni Mitchell and John

Harney have created opposite impressions of the seagull. Select any poem in this book and try to create an opposing impression with your own poetry.
Night in the City
5. Both *Night in the City* and *Lines Composed Upon Westminster Bridge* present pictures of beauty. Yet both portraits admit a sense of the ephemeral. They seem to be only temporary situations. Why is this feeling more poignant in the Mitchell lyric than in Wordsworth's sonnet?

Section 5: John Lennon and the Beatles
A Day in the Life
1. a) Arrange each of the works in this unit into a "scale of bitterness", beginning with the least negative (in your opinion) and ending with the most pessimistic.
b) What are the elements of poetry and lyric that you chose as your criteria for creating the "scale" in (a)?
c) To which of the poems in the unit is *A Day in the Life* most similar: i) in narrative style, ii) in diction, iii) in attitude.
d) The significance of many of the lyrics discussed so far in this book depends at least primarily on the fact that they are sung. Yet *A Day in the Life* can stand strictly as poetry and lose little or no impact. Why is this so?
Eleanor Rigby
2. a) What factors of content and style make the emotional expression of *Eleanor Rigby* less intense than that of the poetry in the unit?
b) Do all the selections in this unit suggest that sexuality might be an antidote for loneliness?
c) Examine each of the works in the unit to discover whether there is any common pattern of imagery, situation, character, and so on, used in the portrayal of loneliness.
Lucy in the Sky with Diamonds
3. a) Show how each selection in the unit attempts to affect as many of the physical senses as possible.
b) If the kind of juxtaposition used in the lyric and poems of this unit achieves such pleasant freshness and vitality, why don't all lyricists write this way?

Section 6: Bruce Cockburn
Bird Without Wings
1. How does Cockburn make explicit through metaphor the kind of love that he wants? Compare the use of metaphor in *Bird Without Wings* with that of Penelope Schafer's *A Sunlight Myth*.
The View from Pompous Head
2. Compare the narrative styles of *The View from Pompous Head* and *To Marguerite*. What are the differences in effect, achieved by such things as physical perspective, emotional involvement, and singing versus speaking?

Section 7: William Hawkins
Cotton Candy Man
1. a) Compare Shelley's use of contrast with Hawkins' in *Cotton Candy Man*. Which in your opinion is more effective?
b) What is the difference between what Shelley seems to want and what Hawkins is looking for? Which desire is the more responsible and mature?
Gnostic Serenade
2. a) When you compare Hawkins' lyric with the two sonnets, the latter seem rather stiffly formal and uninviting. Yet, for generations the sonnet was the traditional form for expressing thoughts of love. Can you account for this?
b) Show that despite the differences in idiom and diction between Meredith's sonnet and Hawkins' *Gnostic Serenade* both selections convey an impression of helplessness not found in Drayton's *Farewell to Love*.

Section 8: Jim Morrison and the Doors
The End
a) When Morrison's lyrics are coupled with their music, the result is a "soul" experience. Because of this, is Morrison's message more effective than Whitman's in *Native Moments*, or *Darest Thou*

Now O' Soul? Does *The End* have more impact than Buckley's *Goodbye and Hello?*
b) All of the selections in this section seem to share an element of obscurity. Why? Is obscurity necessary for a message of this kind?
c) Explain the particular techniques employed by each writer to illustrate the common theme of "personal liberation".
d) Consider whether any of the selections in this section achieves an effect, not through any specific technique, but through the total impact of a series of obscure but seemingly related images.

Section 9: Jerry Moore
Ballad of Birmingham
1. a) Point out the various levels of irony in the poems of this unit. Which selection, in your opinion, is the most bitter?
b) Using a tape recorder, prepare a number of different readings of Hughes' *Birmingham Sunday.* Compare the best of these readings with Jerry Moore's lyric. Which has the greater impact?
c) Explain how the simplicity and concrete detail in these selections can portray a complicated subject so vividly.
d) On what bases could you compare Kaufman's *Benediction* with Whitman's *Thou Mother With Thy Equal Brood?* (Section 2, Pete Seeger).
Life Is a Constant Journey Home
2. a) Compare the philosophy expressed by Jerry Moore in *Life Is a Constant Journey Home* with that expressed by the Beatles in *A Day in the Life* (Section 5, John Lennon and the Beatles).
b) Are the themes expressed in Jerry Moore's *Life Is a Constant Journey Home* and *This Is My Time* contradictory or complementary?
This Is My Time
3. Each of the selections in this unit presents an attitude to life, a means of dealing with existence. Determine carefully what this philosophy is in each poem; then, by any available means, try to capture and present a visual expression of these themes.

Section 10: The United States of America
The Metaphysical Circus
1. a) The selections here deal with a similar theme, but *Metaphysical Circus* and *Bagpipe Music* use a simple metre and rhyme, and straightforward detail, whereas *Plea* and *Drugstore* are written in a more complicated form of free verse and use more involved imagery. Is one method more effective than the other?
b) Explain how Ferlinghetti in *A Coney Island of the Mind No. 17,* and Marshall in *Finis Carnivalis,* use the circus image to gain a powerfully ironic effect.
c) Select three or four aspects of modern life about which you have strong, critical feelings. Try to express these poetically, using a free verse style. Then if you can, present the same points in simpler diction, but in a definite metre and rhyme. If you are successful, try to estimate which task was easier, and which poem is more effective.
Stranded In Time
2. The range of emotions evoked by the selections in this unit runs from sadness to real fear. Where does each poem fit into such a scale? Explain why your choices might suggest as much about yourself as they do about the poems.

Section 11: Robin Williamson
The Mad Hatter's Song
a) In experiencing the song and the poems, one may seem more effective than the others. How can we account for this fact?
b) What controls can be found in these wildly imaginative projections?
c) Writers who have answers to both these questions might then test them out by attempting to write some surrealist verse themselves.

Section 12: Myth and *The Ballad of Frankie Lee and Judas Priest*
1. After listening to *The Ballad of Frankie Lee and Judas Priest,* as well as to other Dylan songs, would you agree with the premise that these works have a *physical* effect on the listener as well as an intellectual one? If you agree, explain how this is achieved? If you do not sense this feeling, and yet are aware that others do, attempt to explain your own reaction.

2. a) Can the "ritual" effect, as explained in the introduction, be achieved by reading poetry silently?
b) Read sections of *Song of the Broken Giraffe* aloud. Then read aloud in unison with ever-increasing groups; change tempo; alter pitch. Does your impression of the poem change during the readings?
c) Compare the feelings generated by some of the readings with the lyrical presentation of Dylan's songs.

3. Point out how both *Frankie Lee and Judas Priest* and *Sir Gawaine and the Green Knight* employ traditional ideas and "timeless" allusions.

4. Hopkins' *Carrion Comfort* is very much like the lyric in technique and idea; yet it utterly lacks any of the "tribal" aspect of communication described in the introduction. Discuss.

5. Point out how the poems associated with the lyric in this section illustrate other treatments of the basic issues of faith, surrealism, and myth, which operate in the song.

Section 13: Buffy Sainte-Marie
The Universal Soldier

1. a) Who makes the stronger protest: Buffy Sainte-Marie with her *Universal Soldier*, or E. E. Cummings with his *particular* soldier, Olaf? Justify your choice by reference to specific techniques as well as general content.
b) Is Cummings' poem an answer to the proposal made in the lyric, or is it another view of the same problem that the lyric presents?

2. What statement about war or militarism does each writer make in this unit? Explain how the imagery of each work supports that statement.

3. Examine the form and structure of each of the poems in this unit, and try to discover whether:
a) form and structure are vital to the creation of mood;
b) irregular form and structure create an angrier feeling than regular style is able to.

4. Is Thomas Hardy's *The Man He Killed*, in fact, an anti-war poem?

5. After reading the brief account of Alan Seeger's death in the biography section of this volume, what additional level of meaning is given to *I Have A Rendezvous With Death*?

My Country 'Tis of Thy People You're Dying

6. Using the two selections in this unit as a starting point, prepare a brief anthology of poems on the subject of the Indian in North America, using poems from any source you have available. For the anthology, write a preface which explains the reasons for your selections.

Discography

Black Is the Color
Joan Baez,
Joan Baez in Concert,
Vanguard VSD-2123

The Cherry Tree Carol
Joan Baez,
Joan Baez: Volume 2,
Vanguard VSD-2097

Johnny, I Hardly Knew Yeh
The Clancy Brothers,
*The Clancy Brothers and
Tommy Makem,*
Tradition TLP 1042;
Tommy Makem,
*The Clancy Brothers and
Tommy Maken:
Hearty and Hellish!,*
Columbia CS 8571

Stackerlee
Dave Van Ronk,
Dave Van Ronk: Folksinger,
Prestige 7527

Follow the Drinkin' Gourd
Pete Seeger,
I Can See a New Day,
Columbia CS 9057;
Theodore Bikel,
From Bondage to Freedom,
Elektra EKS 7200

John Henry
Sonny Terry and Brownie McGhee,
Shouts and Blues,
Fantasy 3317;
*Brownie McGhee and
Sonny Terry Sing,*
Folkways Records NYFW 2327;
*Big Bill Broonzy Sings
Folk Songs,* Folkways FA 2328

Woman Blue
Judy Roderick, *Woman Blue,*
Vanguard 79197

Death Don't Have No Mercy
in This Land
Rev. Gary Davis,
Rev. Gary Davis at Newport,
Vanguard 73008

My Father's Mansions
Pete Seeger,
*Waist Deep in the Big Muddy
and Other Love Songs,*
Columbia CS 9505

Oh, Had I a Golden Thread
Pete Seeger, *Rainbow Quest,*
Folkways FA 24543

Talking Union
Pete Seeger, *Talking Union,*
Folkways 5285

Big Muddy
Pete Seeger,
*Waist Deep in the Big Muddy
and Other Love Songs,*
Columbia CS 9505

Who Knows?
Pete Seeger, *Young vs. Old,*
Columbia CS 9873

Goodbye and Hello
Morning Glory
No Man Can Find the War
Once I Was
Tim Buckley, *Goodbye and Hello,*
Elektra EKS 7318

Marcie
Michael from Mountains
Nathan La Franer
Song to a Seagull
Night in the City
Joni Mitchell, *Joni Mitchell,*
Reprise S 6293

A Day in the Life
The Beatles, *Sgt. Pepper's
Lonely Hearts Club Band,*
Capital S-MAS 2653

Eleanor Rigby
The Beatles, *Revolver,*
Capital S*T 2576

Lucy in the Sky with Diamonds
The Beatles, *Sgt. Pepper's
Lonely Hearts Club Band,*
Capital S-MAS 2653

Bird Without Wings
The View from Pompous Head
Cotton Candy Man
Gnostic Serenade
Three's a Crowd,
Christopher's Movie Matinee,
Dunhill S-50030

The End
The Doors, *Doors,* Elektra 74007

Ballad of Birmingham
Life Is a Constant Journey Home
This Is My Time
Jerry Moore, *Jerry Moore,*
ESP-DISK 1061

The American Metaphysical Circus
Stranded in Time
The Garden of Earthly Delights
United States of America,
United States of America,
Columbia CS 9614

The Mad Hatter's Song
The Incredible String Band,
The 5000 Spirits,
Elektra EKS-74010

The Ballad of Frankie Lee
and Judas Priest
Bob Dylan,
John Wesley Harding,
Columbia CS 9604

Universal Soldier
Buffy Sainte-Marie,
It's My Way!,
Vanguard VSD 79142

My Country 'Tis of Thy
People You're Dying
Buffy Sainte-Marie,
Little Wheel Spin & Spin,
Vanguard VSD 79211

Acknowledgements

For My People by Margaret Walker reprinted by permission of Yale University Press from *For My People*, by Margaret Walker, copyright © 1942 by Yale University Press.

The Man and the Machine by E. J. Pratt reprinted from *Collected Poems* by permission of the Macmillan Company of Canada Limited.

American Gothic: To Satch by Paul Vesey reprinted by permission of the author.

The Negro Mother by Langston Hughes from *Selected Poems*. Copyright © 1959 by Langston Hughes. Reprinted by permission of Alfred A. Knopf, Inc.

I Hereby Swear That to Uphold Your House by Elinor Wylie, copyright 1929 by Alfred A. Knopf, Inc., and renewed 1957 by Edwin Ruberstein. Reprinted from *Collected Poems of Elinor Wylie* by permission of the pulisher.

Do Not Go Gentle into That Good Night by Dylan Thomas reprinted from *Collected Poems* by permission of J. M. Dent & Sons Ltd., the Trustees for the Copyright of the late Dylan Thomas, and New Directions Publishing Corp.

'Butch' Weldy by Edgar Lee Masters reprinted from the *Spoon River Anthology* by permission of the Macmillan Company of Canada Limited, © 1914, 1915, 1942, and Mrs. Edgar Lee Masters.

The Shield of Achilles by W. H. Auden, copyright 1952 by W. H. Auden. Reprinted from *Collected Shorter Poems, 1927-1957*, by permission of Random House, Inc.

I Am Waiting by Lawrence Ferlinghetti reprinted by permission of New Directions Publishing Corp.

The Game by St. Denys Garneau reprinted by permission of F. R. Scott.

Dulce et Decorum Est by Wilfred Owen reprinted from *Collected Poems* by permission of Mr. Harold Owen, Chatto and Windus Limited, and New Directions Publishing Corp.

One Home by William Stafford, first published in *The Hudson Review* Vol. VII, No. 3 (Autumn, 1954) from *The Rescued Year* by William Stafford. Copyright © 1960 by William Stafford. Reprinted by permission of Harper and Row, Publishers.

Effort at Speech Between Two People by Muriel Rukeyser reprinted by permission of the International Famous Agency, Inc. Copyright © 1935 by Yale University; copyright © 1960 by Muriel Rukeyser.

The Coming of the Magi by Raymond Souster reprinted by permission of the author.

War by Langston Hughes from *The Panther and the Lash* by Langston Hughes. Copyright © 1967 by Arna Bontemp and George Houston Bass. Reprinted by permission of Alfred A. Knopf, Inc.

Patterns by Amy Lowell reprinted from *The Complete Poetical Works of Amy Lowell* by permission of the Houghton Mifflin Company.

Tern by John Bruce reprinted by permission of the author.

Nun on a Beach by John Harney reprinted by permission of the author.

Newsreel by C. Day-Lewis reprinted by permission of Harold Matson Company, Inc.

The Legs by Robert Graves reprinted from *Collected Poems 1965* by permission of Collins-Knowlton-Wing, Inc., A. P. Watt & Son, and the author.

Fugal-Chorus by W. H. Auden reprinted from *For the Time Being* by permission of Faber and Faber Ltd.

pity this busy monster, manunkind by E. E. Cummings reprinted by permission of Harcourt, Brace and World, Inc.

A Coney Island of the Mind, No. 8 by Lawrence Ferlinghetti reprinted by permission of New Directions Publishing Corp.

Let Me Tell You a Little Story by W. H. Auden, copyright 1940 and renewed 1968 by W. H. Auden. Reprinted from *Collected Shorter Poems, 1927-1957*, by permission of Random House, Inc.

Secretary by Ted Hughes from *The Hawk in the Rain*. Copyright © 1957 by Ted Hughes. Reprinted by permission of Harper and Row, Publishers.

Acquainted with the Night by Robert Frost from *Complete Poems of Robert Frost*. Copyright 1916, 1928 by Holt, Rinehart and Winston, Inc. Copyright 1944 © 1956 by Robert Frost. Reprinted by permission of Holt, Rinehart and Winston, Inc.

Love in the Asylum by Dylan Thomas reprinted from *Collected Poems* by permission of J. M. Dent and Sons Ltd., the Trustees of the Copyright for the late Dylan Thomas, and New Directions Publishing Corp.

Pied Beauty by Gerard Manley Hopkins reprinted by permission of Oxford University Press.

Snow by Louis MacNeice from *The Collected Poems of Louis MacNeice*, edited by E. R. Dodds. Copyright © The Estate of Louis MacNeice 1966. Reprinted by permission of Oxford University Press, Inc., and Faber and Faber Ltd.

After Great Pain a Formal Feeling Comes by Emily Dickinson reprinted by permission, copyright 1929 © 1957 by Mary L. Hampson.

A Sunlight Myth by Penelope Schafer reprinted by permission of the author.

Catechism by Paul Maurice reprinted by permission of the author.

Empty by Maria Nunez reprinted by permission of the author.

Seasons of the Soul by Allen Tate reprinted from *Poems* by permission of Charles Scribner's Sons.

Index of Themes

Index